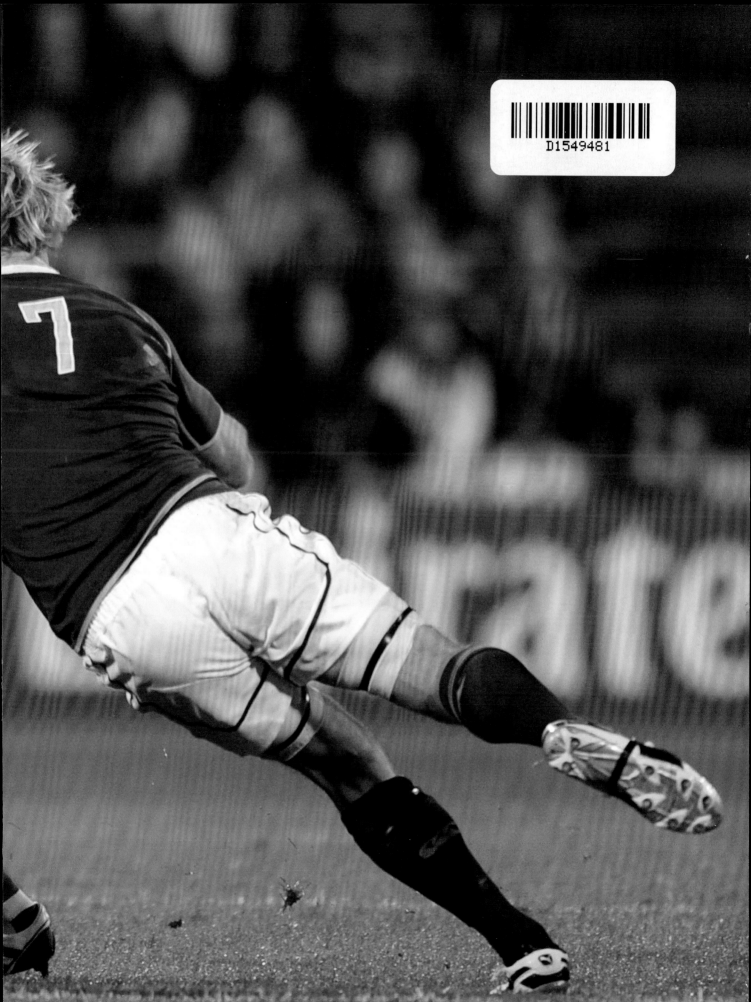

Alun Wyn Jones's
·World Cup Year·

Alun Wyn Jones's

·World Cup Year·

with

Alun Wyn Bevan
and Huw Evans

Published in 2011 by
Gomer Press, Llandysul, Ceredigion, SA44 4JL

ISBN 978 1 84851 428 7

A CIP record for this title is available from the British Library

This book is published with the financial support of the
Welsh Books Council

Printed and bound in Wales at
Gomer Press, Llandysul, Ceredigion

Contents

INTRODUCTION

by Alun Wyn Jones

When I was approached by Alun Wyn Bevan and Huw Evans to be a part of a project to raise funds for the Stepping Stones Appeal at Velindre Hospital, I felt it was my duty to accept but it was also an honour to have been asked. The appeal aims to raise money by all means possible to help patients who suffer from cancer.

The idea behind the book was to provide a personal account of my life as a professional rugby player, and to do so in a very special year – World Cup year. What I didn't know when I accepted the invitation was that this would be no ordinary World Cup campaign for Wales, and that we would reach the semi-finals for the first time since 1987. And even though I know that I went to New Zealand with the sole intention of winning the competition, I think that the team and supporters have a right to feel proud of what has been achieved.

There is a danger that a book like this might mimic the monotony of a professional sportsman's life: 'Monday: Got up. Ate. Trained. Showered. Ate. Slept. Tuesday: Got up. Ate. Trained. Showered. Ate. Slept . . .' But there is more to life than rugby, and I hope that this book shows that there is more to my life than rugby. Indeed I had no choice in this because, from day one, Alun Wyn Bevan was keen to find out about my interests outside rugby, and arranged various events and meetings on my behalf – in his words it was time to 'live the dream'!

It was a mix-up involving our Christian names which first brought Alun Wyn Bevan and me together. First it was Phil Bennett who wrote in his weekly column in the *Daily Mirror* about the exploits of Alun Wyn **Bevan** around the rugby field. Then it was Jonathan Davies's turn whilst commentating on the 2011 France v Wales match at the Stade de France – suddenly it was Alun Wyn **Bevan** who had made a burst for the line! And finally, Radio Cymru's Eleri Siôn, who handed over commentary duties on the Italy v Wales fixture at the Stadio Flaminio in Rome in 2009 to Alun Wyn **Jones**!

I hope you enjoy the read as much I enjoyed the year. Having bought the book, you have helped to support a truly worthy cause.

A Swan in Osprey feathers! The grimace of concentration says it all as I kick intelligently ahead!

JANUARY 2011
A Swig of Heineken and Powerade

January 1

New Year's Day. A lie-in! What a rare luxury! And even better, the Ospreys have a few days off to rest and recuperate.

Mind you, the New Year's Eve celebrations never really took off after a 27–25 defeat at the hands of arch-rivals the Blues. The Ospreys could have won after an excellent second half performance – another few minutes and who knows what would have happened. It's certainly frustrating for all Osprey supporters; the majority couldn't work out why their team was so lethargic during the first forty minutes. I dare say the coaches will spend hours poring over the video evidence on their Hewlett Packards!

As it's Rugby World Cup year, all the international players' preparations will be geared up for the September extravaganza in New Zealand. But there are warning signs already that the heavy work load of the autumn and Christmas period has taken its toll on some of the Ospreys' Welsh hopefuls. I've already played thirteen matches this season so a rest week is a good idea all round.

January 3

Day spent at the Vale of Glamorgan complex at Hensol. The preparation for a mightily important year for the national team has started. Players were all subjected to intense screening procedures which included strength and anaerobic tests, along with the regular medical examinations.

January 5

I attended a sweat session with Powerade Ion 4 – a revolutionary sports drink which keeps players hydrated, helping them play at optimum level. Several film crews present, following the likes of Simon Shaw, Kelly Brown and Luke Fitzgerald. Hope it works for me, not for the others!

January 7

Leinster v Ospreys (*Magners*, Royal Dublin Society ground, Donnybrook)

The coaching team decide on eleven changes from the Blues match with young Justin Tipuric captaining the side for the first time. Leinster fielded a strong XV with O'Driscoll, d'Arcy, Fitzgerald, Sexton, Heaslip and Jennings all included. I watched the match at home – a frustrating exercise but the team could be proud of the overall performance. Again it was a match they could and should have won, but missed kicks proved costly.

Then again, even Carter and Wilkinson have their off days.

Leinster: Fitzgerald, Horgan, O'Driscoll, D'Arcy, McFadden, Sexton, Reddan, Healy, Strauss, Ross, Cullen (c), Toner, Ryan, Heaslip, Jennings Replacements: van der Merwe (40'), Hines (56'), Ruddock (62'), Boss (66'), Nacewa (79')	**Ospreys:** B Davies, Walker, Parker, Beck, Fussell, Biggar, Webb, D Jones, Bennett, Mitchell, Gough, I Evans, Smith, R Jones, Tipuric (c) Replacements: M Davies (62'), Bevington (51'), Griffiths (59'), Goode (70'), J Thomas (70'), Nutbrown (74')

Leinster 15 Sexton (5pg)

Ospreys 10 Tipuric (t), Biggar (1c, 1pg)

Referee: Nigel Owens (WRU)	**Attendance:** 14,876

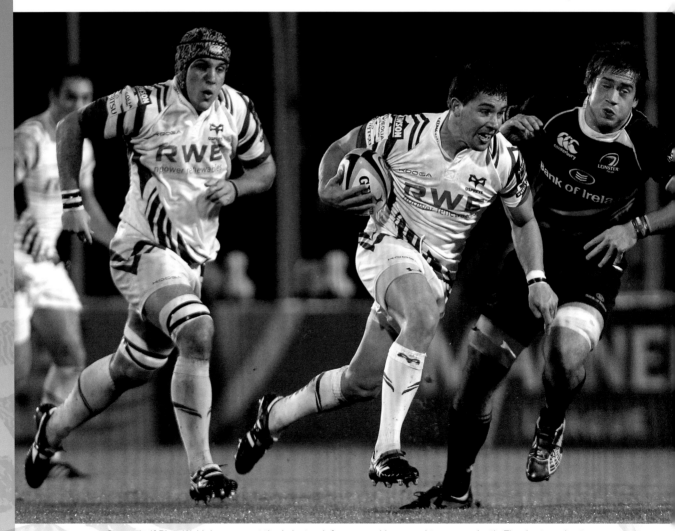

Scrum-half Rhys Webb hovers past the Leinster defence, as skipper and try scorer Justin Tipuric struggles to keep up.

January 11

The Joshua Foundation is the region's chosen charity for the season. It's a charity created in 1998 to provide holidays and worthwhile experiences for children diagnosed with terminal cancer. Along with Richard Hibbard, Paul James, Jerry Collins, Lee Byrne and others, I visited the Sky Ward at the University Hospital in Cardiff. It was a visit much appreciated by all concerned. The children suffering were an inspiration to us all.

January 11–16

The preparations for the vital Heineken Cup fixture at London Irish were fairly routine. Professional sportsmen are, after all, acutely aware of the importance of big matches and are able to adjust to the needs of each fixture. The Ospreys were quietly confident: Irish were out of the competition and had lost ten consecutive matches. But coaches and players prepared meticulously, leaving nothing to chance – we knew that a win would set us up nicely for the remaining group match at the Liberty Stadium against Toulon later in the month. The team came together on the Friday afternoon in a good frame of mind. Could the team erase past disappointments, concentrate on the job in hand and return victorious? Supporters hoped and prayed that the team would learn from previous Heineken encounters like the one against Saracens in 2007.

The players were in good spirits as the coach made its way east along the M4. The team and officials stayed at the ground's hotel – some of the players watched the Scarlets v Leicester match on television (unfortunately Matthew Rees's men failed to match their excellent first-half performance) whilst others either received treatment from our physios, or relaxed in their bedrooms watching DVDs on their computers.

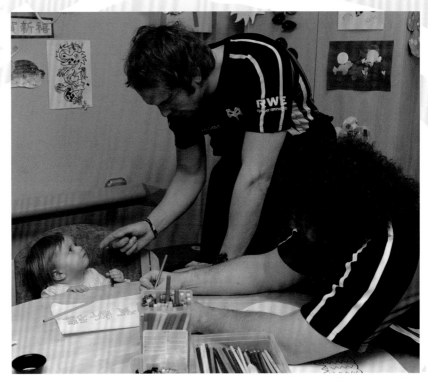

'I told you Adam Jones knew how to hold a pencil.' This visit to University Hospital, Cardiff was an inspiration.

'Just a quick kiss, Tiger!' Scarlets Stephen Jones and Josh Turnbull fight for the affections of Leicester's Ben Youngs

January 17

London Irish v Ospreys (*Heineken*, Madejski Stadium, Reading)

The Ospreys came flying out of their blocks. A perfect start beckoned! An early try would have settled the nerves but it just didn't happen. A second chance materialised but again, for some unknown reason, we blew it. The general feeling inside the ground was that we were bound to win sooner or later, but critics would later hit the nail on the head by accusing us of being 'unable to take advantage of our opportunities'.

Adam Jones's injury was a huge blow – an efficient tight-head prop forward is indispensable, and Adam is one of the finest scrummagers in world rugby.

Tagicakibau and Ojo crossed for two fine tries for the Irish, before a Ryan Lamb penalty proved the final nail in the coffin of a team many considered as favourites to lift the season's Heineken Cup. It proved a long journey back to South Wales; a journey all the way back to the drawing board.

London Irish: D Armitage, Ojo, Seveali'i, Mapusua (c), Tagicakibau (Thompstone 79'), Bowden (Lamb 74'), Allinson, Corbisiero (Murphy 70'), Buckland, Rautenbach (Ion 53'), Kennedy, Garvey, Stowers (Gibson 70'), Hala'ufia. S Armitage (Blaney 72')

Ospreys: B Davies (Byrne 53'), Walker, Bowe, Hook, Fussell, Biggar (Parker 59'), Phillips (Nutbrown 76'), James (D Jones 59'), Hibbard (Bennett 59'), A Jones (Mitchell 40'), R Jones, AW Jones, Collins, J Thomas, Holah (Tipuric 50')

London Irish 24 Tagicakibau (t), Ojo (t), Bowden (3 pg) Lamb (1pg)

Ospreys   12 Biggar (3 pg), Hook (1 pg)

Referee: George Clancy

Attendance: 12,116

London Irish's Sailosi Tagicakibau dives in the corner.

Follow the yellow boots road! Ryan Jones has
London Irish's Darren Allinson in his sights.

January 18, 2011

From THE BEVAN BULLETIN

Captaincy and international duties mean responsibilities. It would have been pleasant for Alun Wyn to relax on the Monday and get the London Irish defeat out of his system. However, David Walsh of *The Sunday Times* had arranged to interview him in the SA1 district of Swansea.

Twelve months previously at Twickenham, Alun's encounter with England's hooker Dylan Hartley had changed the course of the Six Nations. Jones, lying on the ground, had stretched out his foot and tripped the angelic Hartley, resulting in an immediate yellow card from Alain Rolland. During his absence, England scored 17 points as 3–3 became 20–3, and as far as Warren Gatland was concerned, it was what had cost his team victory. Naturally, Walsh wanted to learn more from Wales's second-row forward about the fall-out from the incident. Alun was honest and forthright:

'I was disappointed with what I'd done and with what was said. It's done. You wouldn't normally do that with the coach but in terms of communication in our squad, Warren's style has opened up the channels between us. If he feels he can be that forthright, he's going to accept us coming back to him. Also, if something is said that you don't like, you've got to be man enough to defend yourself.'

David Walsh didn't just concentrate on the one unfortunate incident at Twickers; the positives in Alun Wyn Jones's life far outweigh the negatives. His law degree, his achievements for Wales and the British Lions are all highlighted in an article which portrayed not just a great rugby player but also a rounded individual.

January 19

'Yes for Wales' – I met up with Catrin Evans in Swansea on the Wednesday prior to the Toulon match to offer support for the campaign. Catrin was preparing a You Tube video presentation to drum up support. Some of Wales' biggest stars threw their support behind the campaign chaired by Welsh rugby's chief executive, Roger Lewis, including Shane Williams, Mike Phillips, Robin McBryde and me, all urging the Welsh public to vote 'Yes' on March 3rd.

January 22

Ospreys v Toulon (*Heineken*, Liberty Stadium, Swansea)

Discussion during the days prior to the match centred on the threat from 'you know who'. We wanted to limit the 3-6-9 scenario; that is, infringing in our own half and providing opportunities for Jonny Wilkinson to kick Toulon to victory.

That didn't happen, but Toulon did manage two fine tries via Rory Lamont and Henjak, both converted by the ever dependable Wilkinson, and they were 14–6 ahead at the interval. But the second half was a different story thanks to our concerted effort and the return of the mercurial Shane Williams. A delightful move saw the world's greatest wing three-quarter create space to release Nikki Walker for a vital score. I even got on to the scoresheet as we engineered a deserved, if hollow, 29–17 win.

'You know who'. Toulon's Jonny Wilkinson takes charge.

Ospreys: Byrne, Walker, Parker, Hook, Fussell (S Williams 57'), Biggar (Beck 57'), Webb (Phillips 57'), D Jones (Bevington 50'), Hibbard (Bennett 69'), Mitchell, Gough (Collins 58'), AW Jones (c), R Jones, J Thomas, Tipuric	**Toulon:** Lamont, Lapeyre, Messina, Kefu (El Abd 56'), Brana, Wilkinson (May 56'), Henjak (c) (Magnaval 63'), Taumoepeau (Basteres 58'), Genevois (Ivaldi 61'), Hayman, Suta, Senekal (Chesney 52'), Missoup, Auelua, Sourice

Ospreys 29 Walker (t), AW Jones (t), Hook (2 pg, 2 c), Biggar (3pg)

Toulon 17 R Lamont (t), Henjak (t), Wilkinson (1 pg, 2 c)

Referee: Wayne Barnes (RFU)   **Attendance:** 10,192

The Scarlets' defeat at Perpignan the following afternoon meant that the four Welsh regions had been eliminated from the Heineken Cup, leaving only two Welshmen in with a chance of appearing in the Heineken Cup Final at Cardiff on Saturday, May 15: Northampton's Ryan Powell and referee Nigel Owens.

A lesser spotted Osprey moment: yours truly scoring against Toulon!

January 24

Welsh Six Nations squad announced at mid-day with no real shocks. Five uncapped players included – Josh Turnbull and Rhys Priestland (Scarlets), Ryan Bevington (Ospreys), Scott Andrews (Blues), and Toby Faletau (Dragons). Surprise omission of veteran Martyn Williams but most Welsh fans confidently predict he'll be back to claim his well-deserved hundred caps.

Top table! A brooding Robin McBryde and tight-lipped Warren Gatland let Robert Howley do the talking.

January 26

At a press conference at Portmeirion in North Wales confirmation was received of James Hook's departure to Perpignan after this year's Rugby World Cup. I wonder what the late architect Sir Clough Williams-Ellis would have made of it all? It provides James with an opportunity to play regular rugby at outside half, the position he's coveted since coming onto the scene with Neath RFC some seven years ago. I'm sorry to see him leave the Ospreys but wish him all the best.

Portmeirion to Perpignan. James Hook poses for photographers after his departure for France is announced.

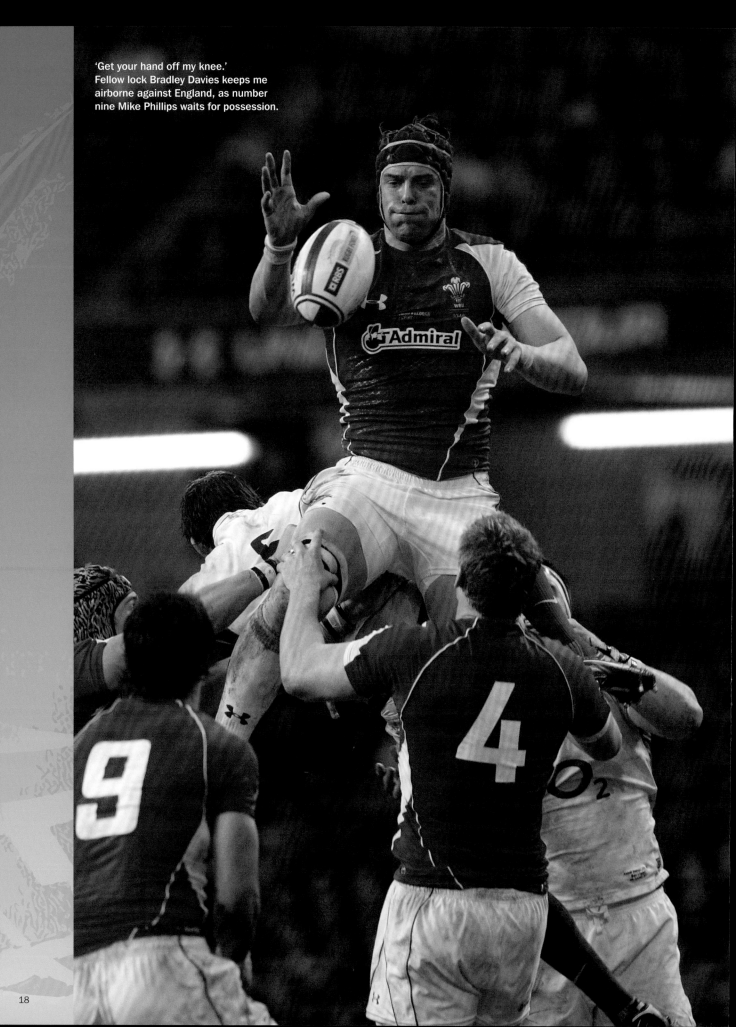

'Get your hand off my knee.'
Fellow lock Bradley Davies keeps me
airborne against England, as number
nine Mike Phillips waits for possession.

FEBRUARY–MARCH

My Six Nations

February 1

Wales's 2008 Grand Slam season included three home matches, which meant we had to win away at Twickenham and Croke Park, and this was quite an achievement. This season we have to travel to Murrayfield, the Stadio Flaminio in Rome and the impressive Stade de France venue in Paris. Some would say it's harder to chisel out three away victories. Some extremely creditable performances against New Zealand in 2010 should, however, serve us in good stead. We certainly need to improve in certain aspects of play but write us off for the Rugby World Cup at your peril! 2011 could be a successful year for Wales.

February 4

Wales v England (Cardiff, 7.45pm)

As players, we were all looking forward immensely to the 2011 Six Nations tournament. The two-week build-up to the England match had gone well; a really good environment with the newcomers providing additional impetus. Subtle changes were implemented by the coaching team with the short, sharp training sessions being well received by squad members. After our shortcomings during the autumn series, a more conscious effort was made to vary our attacking ploys – we wanted to keep possession for prolonged periods. We certainly prepared meticulously for our encounter with the old enemy: we were on edge but also in

Between a rock and a hard place. Playing the role of peacemaker between Craig Mitchell and England's Andrew Sheridan.

a good frame of mind for the battle ahead.

Whatever the pros and cons of a Friday night match, we were aware of a charged atmosphere in the capital city. The noise in the stadium during the hour before kick-off was deafening and certainly had a positive effect on the Welsh players. I was raring to go!

The result was a huge disappointment. We started promisingly enough but failed to score, and international rugby is all about taking opportunities when they arise. Foolishly, we took our foot off the pedal, and allowed Toby Flood to attack two prop forwards before releasing Chris Ashton for that demoralising first try. With England ten points in front after fifteen minutes, they gained in confidence whilst we had a

'Don't stick your tongue out at me!' England's Toby Flood feels the weight of Bradley Davies on his shoulders, and Mike Phillips around his legs.

mountain to climb. We could have retaliated with a try of our own just before half time; Stephen Jones's beautifully judged cross kick was unfortunately knocked on with the line at our mercy.

Worse was to follow. Chris Ashton crossed for his second of the evening and we found ourselves 9–23 in arrears with just twenty minutes remaining. We rallied bravely, and with Morgan Stoddart crossing in the corner, we were within a score of the opposition. Was a win too much to hope for? We certainly matched them up front but found it difficult to create any attacking opportunities. The so-called experts criticised our lateral running and I suppose it's something the coaches have to take on board.

In retrospect I felt that if it had been the third or fourth game of the campaign then we would have won, but there aren't any second opportunities in sport. Frustratingly it was another example of Wales coming off the field within a score of quality opposition. (It's happened against New Zealand on three occasions!) It's difficult to socialise after such a disappointing result, but I had a few words with Joe Worsley, who's a great friend. Can't remember what we talked about though!

Wales: Hook, Stoddart, J Davies, Roberts, Williams, S. Jones, Byrne (67'), Phillips (Peel 69'), James, Rees (Hibbard 70'), Mitchell (Yapp 71'), AW Jones, B Davies, Lydiate (J Thomas 71'), Powell (R Jones 33'), Warburton Unused replacement: Priestland. Yellow card: Mitchell (46)	**England:** Foden, Ashton, Tindall, Hape, Cueto, Flood (Wilkinson 66'), Youngs (Care 62'), Sheridan (Wilson 61'), Hartley (Thompson 69'), Cole, Deacon (Shaw 69'), Palmer, Wood, Easter, Haskell (Worsley 62') Unused replacement: Banahan Yellow card: Deacon (28)

Wales **19** Stoddart (t), S Jones (1c, 3pg), Hook (1pg)	
England 26 Ashton (2t), Flood (2c, 3pg), Wilkinson (1pg)	
Referee: Alain Rolland (Ireland)	**Attendance:** 74,276

The mood was pretty gloomy on the return journey to the Vale of Glamorgan Hotel – I know it's only a game but we realised we had let ourselves and our supporters down badly. That first match in the Six Nations calendar is a vital one to build up hopes and expectations. Frankness and straightforwardness reigned in the days after the defeat. We were honest with ourselves; we don't have to listen to *Scrum V* and newspaper reports to know when we underperform.

Is it a bird, is it a plane . . . No, it's two-try Chris Ashton's modest dive over the line.

February 12

Scotland v Wales (Murrayfield, 5pm)

We knew that we had to be at our very best for the Scottish match. Much was expected of Andy Robinson's men after a stirring performance at the Stade de France. Murrayfield hasn't been a happy hunting ground for Welsh teams in the past. Even John Gwilliam's men, Grand Slam winners in 1950 and 1952, were massacred 19–0 there in 1951. We would need to be streetwise and efficient.

We had a day off on the Sunday, an opportunity to recover from strenuous physical activity, and one which I spent lying down and moving my 120 kilograms as little as possible. I listened to music, so it could have been anything from Lionel Richie and Stevie Wonder to the American rock bands Chicago and Journey. Sometimes such days are spent staring at cringe-factor television programmes like *CSI* and *The Apprentice*.

The No. 10 jersey for the match was handed to James Hook and it was his searing break that set up Shane Williams for yet another international try. When James is at his best, the pulse of the game changes, and his uncanny judgement put us in the right mood during those opening exchanges. Indeed we held the upper hand throughout, never allowing Scotland opportunities to control for any length of time. Even when we were down to thirteen men, our discipline and control was pretty impressive. This was a comprehensive victory. After the defeat against England, we had managed to recover our poise sufficiently to brush aside all Scottish opposition. Although not at our best, we were more than satisfied with the result and with aspects of the performance. We were a happy bunch of individuals, especially Rhys Priestland and Josh Turnbull who won their first international caps. The Welsh fans headed jubilantly for the Princes Street hostelries.

Scotland: Southwell (S Lamont 20'), Walker, Ansbro, De Luca, Evans, Parks, R Lawson (Blair 47'), Jacobsen, Ford (S Lawson 65'), Murray (Low 47'), Hines, Kellock (MacLeod 69'), Brown, Barclay (Rennie 65'), Vernon

Wales: Byrne (Priestland 71'), Stoddart, Roberts, J Davies, Williams, Hook (S Jones 65'), Phillips (Knoyle 71'), James (Yapp 65'), Rees (Hibbard 71'), Mitchell, B Davies, AW Jones (Turnbull 71'), Lydiate (J Thomas 54'), Warburton, R Jones
Yellow cards: B Davies (24'), Byrne (28')

Scotland 6 Parks (2pg)

Wales 19 S Williams (2t), Hook (1c, 4pg)

Referee: George Clancy (RFU)

Attendance: 60,259

Another day at the office.
The world's greatest wing three-quarter, Shane Williams,
scores the first of his two tries against Scotland.

The future's Scarlet. Rhys Priestland (above) and Josh Turnbull are the latest in a long line of Llanelli players to make their international debuts.

February 22

Rugby became an irrelevance as news filtered through of an earthquake striking the Canterbury region of New Zealand's South Island. It affected the country's second most populous city, Christchurch, especially the city centre and the southern suburbs. In total 181 people were killed in the disaster making it the fourth deadliest disaster of any kind in New Zealand's history.

We're all glued to news bulletins whenever countries and individuals are affected by natural or man-made disasters. This was particularly true on this occasion as so many rugby footballers from New Zealand are currently plying their trade here in Wales. It was a trying time for our colleagues who were desperately seeking information on loved ones caught up in the devastation.

February 26

Italy v Wales (Stadio Flaminio, 2.30pm GMT)

Italy had kicked off their Six Nations campaign with an excellent performance against Ireland in Rome. They were extremely unfortunate to lose – yet another last-minute drop goal from Ronan O'Gara deprived them of a well-deserved victory. However, the following week they suffered an embarrassing defeat against England at Twickenham, and it was back to the drawing board for Nick Mallett's men.

We arrived on the banks of the Tiber on the Thursday afternoon and after a leisurely captain's run retired for the evening. On Friday I foolishly decided to stroll around the historic city hoping to see the Colosseum and the Forum, which were within walking distance of our hotel. However, I encountered enthusiastic Welsh supporters eager to know latest titbits from the Welsh camp! Made a mental note to return again to explore this fascinating city.

The pundits all predicted a comfortable win for Wales. But, like many others in the squad, I had been here before, had played at the Stadio Flaminio and come away on the beaten side. We had to be on guard given the strength of the home support and their determination to bounce back after a humbling defeat at Twickers.

'We have lift off!' Ryan Jones and Dan Lydiate support my jump, and help Wales to steal a march on Italy's Martin Castrogiovanni, Santiago Dellape (4) and Sergio Parisse (8).

Stephen Jones, winning his 98th cap, was recalled at outside half after an injury crisis had sidelined centres Jonathan Davies, Andrew Bishop and Tom Shanklin. It was Stephen in fact who reminded us that we have the ability to play a high-risk, high-tempo game incorporating all fifteen players, a brand of rugby which had paid dividends back in 2008. We all sympathised with James Hook having to move into the centre to occupy his third international position in as many games. Personally I feel that we – just like England and Ireland – are fortunate to be in a position to choose between two classy fly halves. James and I won our first caps together in Puerto Madryn, Patagonia, in 2006, and it was great to see him in Rome becoming the youngest ever Welsh player to win fifty caps.

James Hook drops successfully for goal against Italy.

We started promisingly, determined to play a fifteen-man game in the afternoon sunshine, but Parisse's XV made it difficult for us – they scrummaged well and their confidence soared as Canale scored their opening try. Though at one stage we had seemed to be coasting, thanks to two fine tries from Morgan Stoddart and Sam Warburton, they responded with an impressive series of creative attacks. And whilst the result was never in doubt, when Parisse squeezed in at the corner for Italy's second try,

Try-man Sam! Open-side sensation Sam Warburton swoops over for the second Welsh try against Italy.

it meant they were within a score of us and contesting every phase of play with renewed verve and energy. Let's be honest, we were under pressure throughout the second half, but at least had the nous to take advantage of opportunities. James Hook's drop goal allowed us some breathing space at a vital period.

Some would say that the result flattered us and the pundits rightly criticised the team for committing far too many errors and giving away far too many penalties. But Warren Gatland was pleased with the result and reminded us that our Six Nations title hopes were still alive!

Italy: McLean, Masi (Benvenuti 74'), Canale, Sgarbi, Mirco Bergamasco, Burton (Orquera 67'), Semenzato (Canavosio 71'), Perugini (Lo Cicero 40'), Ghiraldini, Castrogiovanni, Dellape, Geldenhuys, Zanni, Parisse (c), Barbieri	**Wales:** Byrne, Stoddart, Hook, Roberts, Williams, S Jones, Phillips, James, Rees (c) (Hibbard 78'), Mitchell, B Davies, AW Jones, Lydiate, R Jones, Warburton

Italy 16 Canale (t), Parisse (t), Bergamasco (2pg)

Wales 24 Stoddart (t), Warburton (t), S Jones (1c, 3pg), Hook (dg)

Referee: Wayne Barnes (RFU)   **Attendance:** 32,000

March 11

For the second time in almost as many weeks, rugby again became an irrelevance. In what proved a devastating day for the Pacific-coast inhabitants of Tohoku off the north east coast of Japan, a powerful earthquake generated a tsunami which in turn swept away everything in its path. To compound matters, a state of emergency was declared at the Fukushima nuclear power plant resulting in the evacuation of thousands of residents.

The earthquake was the fifth largest in the world since 1900 and was nearly 8,000 times stronger than the one which devastated Christchurch, New Zealand, in February. The Japanese Prime Minister, Naoto Kan, said, 'In the 65 years since the second world war this is the toughest and most difficult crisis for Japan.' The death toll reached 15,745 with 5,924 injured and 4,467 missing; 125,000 buildings were damaged and destroyed. Such a disaster puts sport, and indeed most other things, into perspective.

March 12

Wales v Ireland (Cardiff, 5pm)

As a second-row forward, I was looking forward immensely to the Irish match. This wasn't just because we were competing against our Celtic cousins but because of a contest within a contest. With 143 caps between them, the durability of the Irish second-row forwards Donncha O'Callaghan and Paul O'Connell is unquestionable. You look at the last five or six seasons and they've been the most consistent second-row pairing in northern hemisphere rugby.

Both sides were desperate for a victory to keep their Six Nations hopes alive. Amazingly Ireland had only lost one match in Cardiff since 1983 and held an 8–3 lead in Six Nations matches played. I had missed out on the previous season's match at Croke Park due to injury. Two years earlier a late Ronan

Ireland's Donncha o'Callaghan takes me from the vertical to the horizontal.

O'Gara drop goal had secured an Irish Grand Slam, only their second in history, and had moved us from second to fourth in the 2009 Six Nations table.

We spent some time studying various Irish team and individual ploys on our personal computers (our analysis team pick up trends and prepare DVD clips which enable us to concentrate on countering deficiencies). In our training sessions we also focussed on our set pieces, realising that O'Connell's return would strengthen the Irish pack considerably.

The match itself was not a classic but our championship hopes were kept alive by what one journalist described as a 'gritty win' – and I suppose that sums it up perfectly. Wales were led out by fifty-cap men Ryan Jones and Mike Phillips, but after a cautious opening by both teams, it was Ireland who went ahead. Peter Stringer, who had replaced the concussed Eoin Reddan, drew the defence and released Tommy Bowe who created space for Brian O'Driscoll to cross for his record-equalling 24th championship try. It was a timely boost for the visitors but Wales kept plugging away, defending resolutely and never allowed Ireland to break free.

It was Mike Phillips's try halfway through the second half that turned the game. Jonathan Sexton's touchfinder had just landed in Row K of the lower tier's seating area. Meanwhile, the quick-witted Matthew Rees picked up the ball next to him, threw in to Mike who sprinted all of 40 metres to score an opportunist try. The referee Jonathan Kaplan consulted with his assistant Peter Allen who assured him that the ball touched down by the home scrum-half was the same ball that had just been kicked into touch. Poor Mr Allen was wrong about this and will probably suffer nightmares for the next fifty years. However, all teams would have taken advantage of such a situation – Ireland included! O'Driscoll and O'Connell pleaded with the referee to consult the video official but to no avail. (I suppose there'll be a law change prior to the World Cup allowing referees to contact the television official in all matters pertaining to the game. Bring your Thermos Flasks and sandwiches!) Warren Gatland later agreed that it was a poor call. But in fairness, Ireland accepted the decision, even if coach Declan Kidney was far from happy with it. Such decisions in rugby football have to be accepted.

Ireland had a glorious opportunity to win the game in the last minute. O'Driscoll's men needed a converted try for victory but Paddy Wallace veered inside with Keith Earls unmarked outside him. Ronan O'Gara became the fifth man to reach a thousand points in international rugby, joining Jonny Wilkinson, Dan Carter, Neil Jenkins and Diego Dominguez in a rather exclusive club. From a personal point of view, the set pieces went really well. We didn't, however, deal effectively with Ireland's insistence on standing up in the tackle to create a maul. Thankfully, this didn't prove decisive.

Wales: Byrne, Halfpenny, Roberts, J Davies, S Williams, Hook, Phillips, James, Rees (c) (Hibbard 72'), Mitchell (Yapp 13'), B Davies, AW Jones, Lydiate, R Jones (J Thomas 60'), Warburton	Ireland: Fitzgerald (P Wallace 72'), Bowe, O'Driscoll (c), D'Arcy, Earls, O'Gara (Sexton 49'), Reddan (Stringer 1'), Healy, R Best (Cronin 76'), Ross (Court 69'), O'Callaghan (Cullen 76'), O'Connell, O'Brien, Heaslip (Leamy 69'), D Wallace
Wales 19 Phillips (t), Hook (1c, 3pg), Halfpenny (1pg)	
Ireland 13 O'Driscoll (t), O'Gara (1c, 2pg)	
Referee: Jonathan Kaplan (SA)	**Attendance:** 73,856

Second row, second to none.
Bradley Davies and I savour victory
over Ireland (and over O'Connell
and O'Callaghan!)

'Talk to the hand!'
Mike Phillips keeps Ospreys team-mate Tommy Bowe at
arm's length en route to a decisive but controversial try.

March 19

France v Wales (Stade de France, 7.45pm GMT)

Played four, won three – we were on a run and there was no reason why we couldn't go to Paris and do what our predecessors had managed so dramatically in 1999, 2001 and 2005. With Italy's spectacular victory against the *Tricolores* in Rome – and with England having to go to the Aviva Stadium to face an Irish side firing all cylinders – it was mathematically possible for Wales to clinch the title.

We arrived at our hotel near the Champs-Elysées on the Thursday afternoon and on this occasion I decided not to do any sight seeing. With my *Lonely Planet Guide* to Paris left in Swansea, that would have to keep for another day! When you're based at a hotel, the day seems to get longer and longer and we all had to adapt as the kick-off was 8.45pm Paris time. I got up on the Saturday at 10.30am, had some scrambled eggs in the restaurant and went back to bed. I had nothing extravagant for lunch, ventured out for a short walk near Place de la Concorde and then made use of a local team's training pitch. We arrived in good time at the Stade de France in St-Denis, the stadium built for the 1998 Football World Cup, and which gets less intimidating the more you play there.

By kick-off, we all felt reasonably confident, buoyed by Ireland's crushing of England that afternoon, and knowing what we had to do to win the title. Our coaching staff, however, reminded us that France, after their shock defeat against Italy, had a point to prove to their spectators who would be baying for blood were France to underperform again.

We weren't the side which played the previous three games. We didn't keep the ball long enough to score. Occasionally an individual has to carry the can for a defeat – a missed tackle, a dropped pass, poor decision-making etc. The game was littered with basic errors. There were also several 'what if' moments. What if Leigh Halfpenny had avoided Trinh-Duc's ankle tap? What if Jamie Roberts had received a return pass from Jonathan Davies after a threatening run? What if Sam Warburton hadn't been injured, and James Hook's kick hadn't been charged down? And what if the Welsh eight had made their presence felt throughout the evening?

After the final whistle I was interviewed and asked to comment on our disappointing defeat. After a poor performance it's not something you want to do. However, I had to be honest and try to convey the team's feelings:

It's a barren place in the changing room . . . we're an honest bunch . . . this game's going to hurt . . . some harsh words have been spoken . . . we were lethargic; we lacked urgency . . . we've played worse and won . . . we want to be in the top three in the world . . . I have no excuses . . . with three consecutive victories we were quietly confident . . . we won't point any fingers.

We eventually returned to the hotel rather downcast still trying to work out where it all went wrong.

France: Medard, Clerc, Marty, Traille, Palisson, Trinh-Duc, Parra, Domingo, Servat, Mas, Pierre, Nallet, Dusautoir, Bonnaire, Harinordoquy, Replacements: Guirado, Ducalcon, Pape, Lapandry, Tomas, Estebanez, Huget	**Wales:** Byrne, Halfpenny, Roberts, J Davies, North, Hook, Phillips, James, Rees (c), Jones, B Davies, AW Jones, Lydiate, R Jones, Warburton Replacements: Hibbard, Yapp, Thomas, McCusker, Peel, S Jones, Stoddart
France 28 Nallet (2t), Clerc (t), Parra (2c 3pg)	
Wales 9 Hook (3pg)	
Referee: Craig Joubert (SA)	**Attendance:** 79,798

Ball n'all, Imanol!
A bent-double Dan Lydiate gets
to grips with France's Imanol
Harinordoquy, as Ryan Jones
closes in.

Ils ne passeront pas! The French defence proved impregnable at Stade de France, as both Jamie Roberts (below) and I find out

The one that didn't get away.
Leigh Halfpenny is brought to ground
by Francois Trinh-Duc's despairing but
decisive ankle tap.

Hanno Domini!
Osprey centre Hanno Dirksen lords it over the Blues.

MEANWHILE

. . . in the Magners (and LV)

Although I was totally focused on the Six Nations Championship, I hoped to keep track of the Ospreys' progress in the LV Cup and the Magners League. It proved to be a very successful few weeks for the team with the youngsters proving once again how important they are to the region.

January 29

Blues v Ospreys (*LV*, Cardiff City Stadium)

With a sprinkling of internationals in their line-up, the Ospreys won convincingly although it has to be said that both teams were missing key personnel. On this occasion I watched the match on television, one of many different ways of keeping in touch with developments. Coach for the day Filo Tiatia was delighted with the performance describing it as a good exercise. He was particularly pleased with the character displayed when the team was reduced to thirteen men. The competition is an excellent one in terms of player development.

Ospreys coach for the day, Filo Tiatia.

Blues: Fish, Taylor, G Evans, Hewitt (c), H Robinson, Griffin, Downes, T Davies, Dacey, Hobbs, B Griffiths, Cook, Hamilton, Brown, Navidi	**Ospreys:** Prydie, Phillips, Owen, Beck, Dirksen, M Morgan, Webb, D Jones, M Davies, C Griffiths, Goode, I Evans, King, Smith, Tipuric (c)
Replacements: R Williams, Smout, WG John, Hill, Sheppard, L Jones, L Williams, Loxton	Replacements: Bennett, Cross, Taylor, Kelly, Allen, Nutbrown, Isaacs, Flanagan

Blues   **7**   G Evans (t), Griffin (c)

Ospreys 29   penalty try, Allen (t), Dirksen (t), M Morgan (1c, 4 pg)

Referee: Dave Pearson (RFU)   **Attendance:** 10,320

February 6

Ospreys v London Wasps (*LV*, Brewery Field, Bridgend)

A closely fought encounter, featuring an extremely mature defensive display from the young Ospreys. Travelled to Bridgend to support the team and was glad to see an enthusiastic crowd present. Since the Celtic Warriors were disbanded, the Bridgend area has been deprived of top-class rugby at the Brewery Field. Let's hope the Ospreys continue to fly the flag in a part of Wales which has managed to provide a wealth of talent for the national team. We were also glad to see the return of Tom Isaacs after a long lay-off. He was by far the most potent attacker on view and outshone the experienced Wasps combination of Waldouck and Flutey.

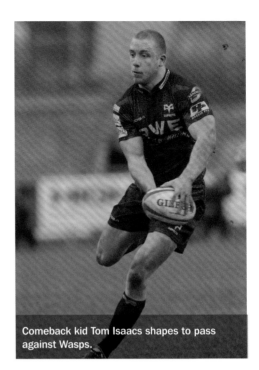

Comeback kid Tom Isaacs shapes to pass against Wasps.

Ospreys: Prydie, Phillips, Isaacs, Owen (Parker 71'), Dirksen, Flanagan (Biggar 60'), Webb (Nutbrown 71'), C Griffiths (Rees 78'), Bennett, Cross (D Jones 48'), Gough (Collins 60'), I Evans, King, Smith, Tipuric (c)	**Wasps:** van Gisbergen (Wallace 45'), Haughton, Waldouck, Flutey, Varndell, Walder, Davies (Holmes 67'), Ruwers (Beech 55'), Ward (c), Broster (Baker 75'), Launchbury (Jones 75'), Cannon, Hart, Betsen, Vunipola, Tchoua
Ospreys 18 Flanagan (4pg), Biggar (1pg, 1dg)	
Wasps 13 van Gisbergen (t), Varndell (t), Walder (1pg)	
Referee: Dean Richards (RFU)	**Attendance:** 4,800

'What's the plan, Dan?' Dan Biggar (left) looks to set up Tom Smith against Ulster

February 13

Ospreys v Ulster (*Magners*, Liberty Stadium)

In an extremely tight finish, the Ospreys managed to neutralise the visitors' South African contingent, and scraped home by a solitary point thanks to Dan Biggar's late penalty goal. At one stage it looked as if we were going to experience a seventh Magners League defeat after trailing 13–0 after twenty minutes. It was a much needed win as things are getting quite congested at the top of the group. Coach Jonathan Humphreys was impressed by the team's never-say-die attitude.

Ospreys: Fussell, Prydie, Parker, Beck, Dirksen, Biggar, Webb, D Jones, Bennett, Griffiths, Gough, I Evans, Smith, Collins (c), Holah
Replacements: Davies, Bevington, Cross, King, Tipuric, Nutbrown, Owen, Isaacs

Ulster: D'Arcy, Gilroy, Spence, Whitten, Danielli, I Humphreys, Pienaar, Young, Brady, Fitzpatrick, Muller (c), Barker, Henry, Faloon, Wannenburg
Replacements: Kyriacou, Cronin, Whitten, Caldwell, Anderson, P Marshall, L Marshall, McIlwaine

Ospreys 23 Holah (t), Biggar (6pg)

Ulster   22 penalty try, I Humphreys (1c, 2pg), Pienaar (3pg)

Referee: Neil Patterson (RFU)   **Attendance:** 5,802

Muller light.
Ulster captain Johann Muller
is lifted easily skywards.

February 19

Benetton Treviso v Ospreys

(*Magners*, Stadio Comunale Monigo)

The Stadio Comunale Monigo has proven to be a difficult place for visiting teams with the Italians claiming some notable Heineken Cup and Magners League scalps there already. However, a polished performance saw us recording five tries on the way to a welcome victory, with the bonus point secured inside fifty minutes.

Nikki Walker, playing only a week after the defeat at Murrayfield, claimed his second hat-trick of the season, while veteran second-row forward Ian Gough went over for his first touchdown ever in Ospreys colours. It was also pleasing for Ospreys and Irish supporters to see Tommy Bowe (below) returning after a month on the sidelines with a knee injury. I followed proceedings via text updates and live feeds on-line.

Treviso: Williams, Nitoglia, Galon, Pratichetti, Sepe, Marcato, Botes, Filippucci, Padro, Vermaak, Van Zyl, A Pavanello (c), Di Santo, Sbaraglini, Rouyet Replacements: Ceccato, Muccignat, Cittadini, E Pavanello, Vosawai, De Jager, Benvenuti, Vilk	**Ospreys:** Fussell, Bowe, Parker, Beck, Walker, Biggar, Webb, D Jones, Bennett, Griffiths, Gough, I Evans, Smith, Collins, Tipuric (c) Replacements: M Davies, Bevington, Cross, Lloyd, King, Nutbrown, Flanagan, Isaacs.

Beneton Treviso 18 Botes (2t, 1c, 2pg)

Ospreys   **34** Walker (3t), Gough (t), Beck (t), Biggar (3c, 1pg)

Referee: John Lacey (IRFU)	**Attendance:** 4,200

Ian Gough, scorer of tries.

February 27

Ospreys v Connacht

(*Magners*, Liberty Stadium)

The Ospreys moved into second position in the Magners League with a comfortable victory over Connacht at the Liberty Stadium. A minute's silence was observed as a mark of respect for the victims of the Christchurch earthquake – such a tragedy puts everything into perspective. It must have been a particularly moving occasion for Connacht and New Zealand Under 20 prop forward Rodney Ah You, who was born and bred in Christchurch.

Replacement hooker, the dependable and everlasting Mefin Davies (below), sealed a valuable bonus point with a try five minutes into injury time but the visitors competed well throughout making it extremely difficult for us to stamp any authority on the contest.

The Ospreys' second try was a beauty which saw Wales wing Tom Prydie sprint down the left touchline after good work from Fussell, Beck and Parker. I followed proceedings closely on my iPhone on the bus back from Cardiff Airport.

Ospreys: Fussell, Prydie, Parker, Beck, Dirksen, Biggar, Webb, D Jones, Bennett, Griffiths, Gough, I Evans, Smith, Collins, Tipuric (c)
Replacements: Bishop, Bevington, M Davies, Cross, King, Lloyd, Isaacs, Flanagan

Connacht: Duffy, Tuohy, Ta'auso, Nathan, Carr, Keatley, F Murphy, Wilkinson, Flavin, Hagan, Swift, McCarthy, A Browne, Ofisa, O'Connor (c)
Replacements: Matthews, Nikora, Willis, Loughney, Rodney Ah You, Upton, D Murphy, McComish

Ospreys   33 Parker (t), Fussell (t), Prydie(t), M Davies (t), Biggar (2c, 2pg, 1dg)

Connacht 18 O'Connor (t), Swift (t), Nikora (c), Keatley (2pg)

Referee: Stefano Penne (Italy)   **Attendance:** 5,851

Beck off!
Ashley Beck seems determined
to break Troy Nathan's tackle.

Up 'em and Adam!
British Lion tight-head prop Adam Jones has a breather
during his return to Osprey colours against Glasgow.

Tom Smith slides over against Glasgow.

March 5

Ospreys v Glasgow Warriors

(Magners, Liberty Stadium)

This was a really encouraging performance by the Ospreys – the forwards dominated play throughout, providing ample possession for the halfbacks who in turn brought the best out of a potent back line. The win certainly boosted our play-off aspirations. Dan Biggar was at his majestic best, answering his critics with a display which augurs well for the future. It was great to see Adam Jones back on the bench – the prop forward desperately waiting for his opportunity to prove to Warren Gatland that he's in good shape and ready to return to the national fifteen.

Glasgow were 17–0 down after twenty minutes play and the match as a contest was all but over. The Ospreys were adventurous in attack and stubborn in defence. Glasgow flyer van der Merwe was in the act of scoring when Ashley Beck appeared from nowhere and prevented the wing three-quarter from scoring with a magnificent tackle. The Ospreys strength in depth was in evidence with Prydie, Beck, Isaacs, Dirksen, Bevington and Tipuric all contributing to an outstanding all-round display.

The highlight of the evening was a never-to-be-forgotten length of the field movement involving Isaacs, Duncan Jones, Fussell and the lively Ashley Beck. It was the youngster from Skewen who eventually touched down for a try which deserves to be in the reckoning for the Magners League try of the season. The evening's only damper was a serious injury to Tom Prydie who was helped off the field with knee ligament damage.

Ospreys: Fussell, Prydie (Isaacs 54'), Parker, Beck, Dirksen, Biggar (Flanagan 72'), Webb (Nutbrown 72'), Bevington (D Jones 59'), Hibbard (Bennett 46'), Griffiths (A Jones 58'), Gough (King 68'), Evans, Smith, Thomas (Collins 58'), Tipuric (c)

Glasgow: Hogg (Aramburu 67'), O'Hare, Murchie, (Stortoni 57'), van der Merwe, Weir (Pyrgos 54'), Gregor (c), Grant, Thomson (MacArthur 54'), Kalman (Tkachuk 21'), Muldowney (Harley 46'), Ryder, Eddie (Beattie 48'), Wilson, Forrester.

Ospreys 37 Biggar (t, dg, 3pg), penalty try, Smith (t), Beck (t), Collins (t)

Glasgow 6 Weir (2pg)

Referee: Alan Folzone (Italy)　　　　**Attendance:** 5,642

March 26

Edinburgh v Ospreys (*Magners*, Murrayfield)

We travelled up to the Scottish capital in buoyant mood with the return of our international contingent who were keen to see the team maintaining their push for a Magners League play off position. It augured well – the preparatory work had been thorough and we had what seemed to be a loaded bench. It was a rather unreal scenario. With room for over 80,000, there were only 1,500 present!

We started promisingly thanks to two early Dan Biggar penalties and when Dan ran over for the game's first try it seemed as if we had the measure of our opposition. However, Edinburgh responded and following a series of attacks, man-of-the-match David Denton was within a whisker of opening their try account but the television match official ruled a knock-on as he crossed the goal line. The home side continued to impress and eventually claimed their first try when full-back Jim Thompson plunged over. Laidlaw's conversion made it 13–10 to the Ospreys at the interval.

'And for my next trick . . .' Dan Biggar juggles one-handed as Edinburgh's Jim Thompson (number 15) and I (right) look on.

The second half was dominated by Edinburgh. Even when Esteban Lozada was yellow carded, they controlled play against a regrouped Ospreys XV. A magnificent Tim Visser try (he scored a hat-trick in the corresponding fixture last season) put Edinburgh 20–16 in front – several players handled before Scott MacLeod released Visser. The 'Flying Dutchman' glided past the defence for what proved to be a vital score.

Edinburgh: Thompson, Webster, Cairns, King, Visser, G Laidlaw, M Blair, Traynor, Kelly (c), Young, MacLeod, Lozada, McKenzie, Denton, Newlands
Replacements: Walker, Hislop, Gilding, Turnbull, Dewar, L Jones, D Blair, Brown

Ospreys: Fussell, Bowe, Parker, Beck, Walker, Biggar, Webb, D Jones, Bennett, A Jones, Gough, Evans, Smith, R Jones, Tipuric (c)
Replacements: Hibbard, Bevington, Griffiths, AW Jones, Collins, Isaacs, Hook, Bishop

Edinburgh 23 Thompson (t), Visser (t), Laidlaw (2c, 3pg)

Ospreys 16 Biggar (t, c, 3pg)

Referee: Dudley Phillips (IRFU) | **Attendance:** 1,500

POSTSCRIPT

March also saw the retirement of one Wales's most promising back-row forwards, one who had been on the verge of being capped during the 2009/10 season.

It's not a pleasant experience to be told at the age of 24 that one's career as a professional rugby player is at an end. Ben Lewis had originally been stretchered off the field on September 25, 2010 in a Magners League match against Aironi at the Liberty Stadium, but he had managed to recover from the hyper-flexion injury in the neck which had caused a slight bulge in the disc. He bravely returned to playing action with Swansea RFC in a Premiership match at Tonmawr five months later, but unfortunately suffered a recurrence of the same injury.

We were all saddened by his premature departure. However, Ben was one of the lucky ones and a shining example to others because he had also completed his academic studies at Swansea University and was able to take advantage of his degree and think in terms of forging a career in another field. We wish him well.

One of Wales's most promising back-row forwards, Ben Lewis, now sadly retired.

'The name's Jones. Alun Wyn Jones.'
Test-driving an Aston Martin in the Brecon Beacons.

JAMES BOND

. . . for a day

All I did was let slip to Alun Wyn Bevan that – if I had more spare time – I wouldn't mind driving a fast car. And, lo and behold, he'd set up a test drive with Aston Martin for me! What's more, this too would be part of the fundraising venture for the Cancer Research Centre at Velindre in Whitchurch.

I'm not used to getting up at 7.30am on my day-off. But when my date with petrolhead destiny arrived, the signs were postitive ones – it was a glorious day for a drive, Swansea Bay looking quite spectacular and the bacon rolls at the Nant Ddu Lodge Hotel extremely tasty. Having heard all about the car around the breakfast table (the Aston Martin representative, Gareth Criddle, from the Stratstone garage in Cardiff, was quite passionate about the vehicle), it was time to experience it first hand. I was smitten from the word go; it really was a stunning piece of engineering.

But how on earth would a 6ft 7in, 120 kilogram (18st 12lb) second-row forward fit into what seemed a claustrophobic cockpit? As it turned out, I slid in with ease, and, with the sun blazing overhead, it was time to dispense with the jacket, reach out for the Oakleys and press the convertible release button. Before us lay the Brecon Beacons National Park, and we were about to explore it in some style.

I must have impressed Gareth (who was seated nervously beside me) with my wealth of information . . . 'It all began with a small, fast sports car built by Banford and Martin in 1914. The company was re-incorporated in 1947 as part of the David Brown group becoming immediately successful.' Enough! Enough! I was not the only one who seemed mightily impressed with the performance – even the sheep courteously moved aside at the sound of the V8 engine. However, at a constant (and legal) speed, I wasn't even aware the engine was ticking over. Aston Martin constantly reminds its customers that it combines three important elements: power, beauty and soul, and I was in complete agreement with their assessment.

I was in my seventh heaven and would have loved to have said to Gareth, 'I'll take it with me!' Another thing I didn't tell him was that it had taken me four attempts to pass my driving test!

Before I hang up my boots, I'd love to be able to experience a season or two playing for one of those French clubs bordering the Mediterranean. But you wouldn't catch me commuting back to Wales on a low-cost airline. Oh no! I'd insist on driving back in my Aston Martin, and be known throughout Europe as 005!

Lifting in the line-out was never this elaborate. Swansea Sirens proved inspirational cheerleaders at the Welsh varsity match.

Two Tales of Two Cities

March 30

Cardiff University v Swansea University (Millennium Stadium)

The Welsh Varsity match was not only a great occasion for the 12,000 spectators present (the majority vociferous students who could have been dressed for an end-of-season Mardi Gras) but also a huge thumbs-up for rugby football. It really was a spectacular contest and I was delighted to have been there. Some of you should have responded to the re-tweeted ticket offers on Twitter:

> @ I'm trying to get rid of 3 tickets for the Cardiff v Swansea varsity match tomorrow for FREE!

Rugby analysts everywhere continue to champion statistics that prove that possession and dominant set pieces are the paving stones of victory. But this match suggested that interpreting such statistics is actually like pulling rabbits out of a hat. As someone once said, you could present a statistic as fact even if it was an illusion. Indeed, the first half facts and figures for this particular match must have caused embarrassment to all statisticians – Cardiff totally dominated proceedings, winning what must have been 90% possession, but were frustrated in their attempts to cross the try line by a determined Swansea XV who tackled and defended resolutely. And when they managed to get their hands on the ball, they caused panic. Unbelievably, Swansea led 14–6 at half time thanks to excellent tries from Henry Boot and scrum-half Tom Rowlands.

As a former Swansea student who played in the corresponding 2005 encounter, I enjoyed proceedings from the hospitality box. The WRU hierarchy must have been impressed with the numbers present and the quality of play – even the great Gerald Davies had a smile on his face! The students have packed the Liberty Stadium and the Arms Park in the past, and it was quite an effort to stage the fixture at the Millennium Stadium. Let's hope that after the carnival atmosphere of this spectacular match that it will become a key date in the Welsh rugby calendar.

Swansea University celebrate victory over arch-rivals Cardiff, as captain Rhodri Clancy holds the cup aloft.

The second half proved just as exciting as the first with both teams claiming two tries apiece, Swansea through Dan George and a superb individual effort from outside half Aled Lewis, whilst Jake Cooper-Woolley and James Reeves crossed for Cardiff. Premier South A runners-up Swansea deservedly won by 28–18. Praise also to S4C who decided to televise the match, allowing rugby followers throughout the digital world to share in the fun.

Cardiff University: Coombes, Chatwin, Greendale, Wardle, W Jones, Pimlow, Schropfer, Lewin, Grimstone, Cooper-Woolley, Murphy, Bray, Huntley, Hendry, D Lewis
Replacements: Reeves, R Price, Porter, G Jones, Wood, Casells, S Morgan.

Swansea University: M Jones, D Evans, C Evans, Chance, R Thomas, A Lewis, Rowlands, O'Sullivan, Clancy (c), I Williams, M Thomas, Boot, Bray, Beer, D George
Replacements: Apsee, Littlehales, G George, S Lewis, Lakin, Szabo, Barley, Smart

Cardiff University **18** Cooper-Woolley (t), Reeves (t), Pimlow (1c, 2pg)

Swansea University 28 Boot (t), Rowlands (t), D George (t), A Lewis (t, 4c)

Referee: Nigel Owens (WRU) | **Attendance:** 12,000

Swansea scrum-half Aled Lewis stretches for the try line.

April 2
Ospreys v Blues (*Magners*, Liberty Stadium)
High Noon! Gun fight at the O.K. Corral! With both teams pushing for top four places in the Magners League, this was a crucial game for both Welsh regions. It proved to be a huge disappointment for all concerned; certainly not a game for the connoisseurs with defensive formations and goal kickers the only winners. But let's be honest – how many derby matches in days of old between Neath and Aberavon, Llanelli and Swansea, Pontypridd and Bridgend, Cardiff and Newport were scintillating affairs. From what I've been told they were often rotten, roguish matches with tries and attacking moves at a premium.

We certainly started purposefully moving the ball at every opportunity and managed to disrupt the Blues pack in the first few scrummages, but as the game developed we seemed to cancel each other out. We always had our noses in front but to be fair to the Blues, their never-say-die attitude resulted in spoils being shared.

Ospreys: Fussell (Byrne 47'), Bowe, Parker, Hook, Walker, Biggar, Webb (Phillips 54'), James (Bevington 75'), Bennett (Hibbard 50'), A Jones, AW Jones (c), Evans, R Jones, Collins, Tipuric

Blues: Fish, Halfpenny, Laulala, Roberts, James, Parks, Rees, Felise, G Williams, Andrews (Hobbs 53'), B Davies, Tito (c) (Paterson 53'), Pretorius, Rush, M Williams

Ospreys 21 Biggar (5pg, 1dg), Hook (1dg)

Blues **21** Parks (5pg, 2dg)

Referee: Christophe Berdos (FFR)

Attendance: 11,619

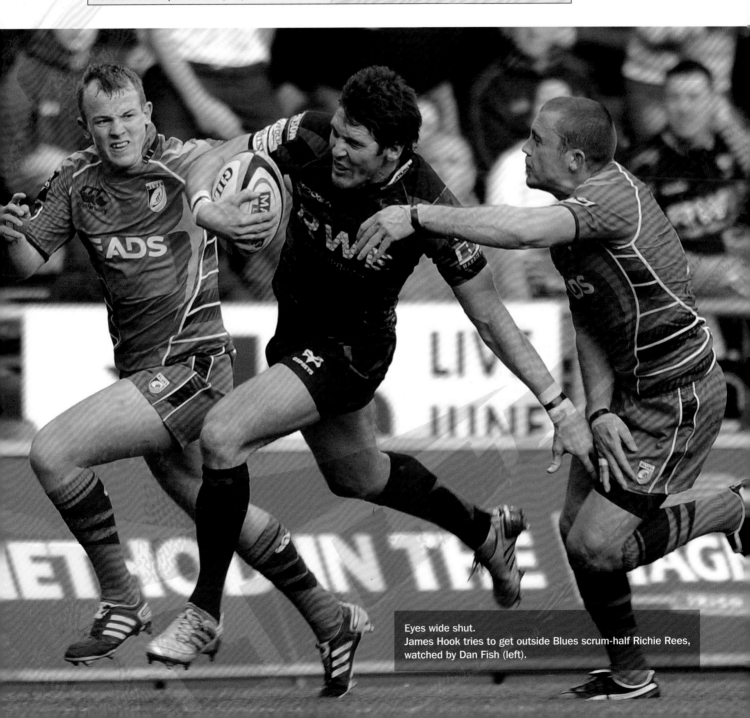

Eyes wide shut.
James Hook tries to get outside Blues scrum-half Richie Rees, watched by Dan Fish (left).

In his Toulouse colours, Gareth Thomas, one of a number of Welsh players to have flourished in the French *Championnat*.

Should I stay or should I go?

April 11, 2011

From THE BEVAN BULLETIN

The exodus of leading Welsh players to France was halted today when Alun Wyn Jones agreed a new three-year contract with the Ospreys. He stays put for the time being which is great news for the region's supporters and for Warren Gatland whose diktat that home based players would receive preferential treatment has not influenced James Hook, Lee Byrne, Gavin Henson and possibly Mike Phillips who take flight to France after this year's Rugby World Cup in New Zealand. There had been strong rumours that Alun would also be tempted to succumb to the euro magnet and join Clermont Auvergne, but he eventually rejected the undoubted interest from the Massif Central club.

Forwards coach Jonathan Humphreys was particularly pleased with the news, 'It's a huge boost that Alun, one of the world's leading second-row forwards has committed his future to the region. He is integral to where we want to take the Ospreys. He is captain for a reason – he demands high standards of himself and his colleagues, is ambitious and has an innate desire to succeed.'

His decision is a massive boost for Welsh rugby. In the press conference at the Liberty Stadium, Alun was delighted that the two parties had come to an agreement:

It has taken longer than anticipated to complete everything but I have never really wanted to play anywhere else and have never said otherwise. It's flattering to have interest from France and offers from other clubs, but I'm conscious that grass isn't always greener on the other side. The evolution taking place at the Ospreys is very positive, we've got an amazing depth of talent, and I'm extremely excited about the next three years. We might not have made into it this season's Heineken Cup quarter finals but we're the current Magners League Champions and are on the verge of making the breakthrough expected of us. The management board, the coaching staff and the players are on the same wavelength which heralds a promising future.

Gavin Henson in Toulon colours, briefly.

Two Dragons play Tom and Jerry.
Luke Charteris (left) and Lloyd Burns seem
to have Jerry Collins in their clutches.

APRIL-MAY

A last round of Magners

April 15

Dragons v Ospreys (*Magners*, Rodney Parade, Newport)

To the home fans and any neutral observers, this eighty-minute affair was a match to remember and a credit to the Magners League. The Dragons roared into a 21-point lead early in the second half with three tries in quick succession. However the Ospreys riposte meant that the match was finely poised right up to the final whistle. I'm convinced a further five minutes play would have resulted in an away win!

We were on the back foot from the word go when some fine inter-passing between Ashley Smith and the highly promising Toby Faletau saw the centre three-quarter run in from close range. However, we retaliated in fine style when Ryan Jones took advantage of James Hook's ball skills to cross in the corner. The atmosphere was highly charged and the Ospreys realised that the Dragons meant business under their newly appointed coach, Darren Edwards, a former scrum-half at Rodney Parade. Indeed, they should have increased their lead when Tovey's beautifully weighted kick was manna from heaven for the dangerous Aled Brew. He raced away but overran the ball and the opportunity was lost.

The Ospreys defence, which has been rock solid throughout the season, was tested on numerous occasions and was found wanting from time to time especially during a fifteen-minute period at the start of the second half. A defensive error let in Aled Brew for a gift of a try. Brew's second score was fortuitous when Tovey's kick rebounded to the outside half who immediately fed the Swansea Valley wing three-quarter who sprinted impressively for the score. We were trailing 32–11 but responded encouragingly with man-of-the-moment James Hook, who had been moved to outside half after Biggar's departure, instrumental in a remarkable turnaround. He created a try for Tommy Bowe and then put in a measured crosskick for Nikki Walker to run in unopposed. The final few minutes with the Ospreys just four points in arrears proved frenetic but the Dragons, it has to be said, held out for a thoroughly deserved win – the first under Darren Edwards's leadership.

A wry smile from Tommy Bowe as Dragons' Aled Brew celebrates the first of his two tries.

Dragons: Harries (M Jones 10'), Hughes, Riley, Smith (c), A Brew, Tovey, W Evans, Price (Gustafson: temp 27-34'), Burns (S Jones 69'), Castle (Way 73'), Coombs (L Evans 63'), A Jones, Lydiate (Bearman 66'), Faletau, G Thomas

Ospreys: Byrne, Bowe, Bishop (Fussell 60'), Hook, Walker, Biggar (Parker 60'), Webb (Isaacs 55'), James (Bevington 55'), Bennett (Hibbard 48'), A Jones (Griffiths 55'), R Jones (Gough 50'), AW Jones (c), Smith, Collins, Holah (Tipuric 55')

Dragons 32 Brew (2t), Smith (t), L Evans (t), Tovey (1c, 2pg), M Jones (2c)

Ospreys 28 R Jones (t), Bowe (t), Walker (t), Hook (2c, 1pg), Biggar (2pg)

Referee: Nigel Owens (WRU)   **Attendance:** 5,496

Dragons skipper Ashley Smith gets on the scoresheet.

'How's this for an Irish jig?' Munster's Donnacha Ryan and John Hayes are rooted to the spot by Adam Jones's dancing feet.

April 23

Ospreys v Munster (*Magners*, Liberty Stadium)

It was that man . . . again! When rugby historians run their rule over this particular era, Ronan O'Gara will undoubtedly be championed for his pivotal role in the green of Ireland and the red of Munster. His penalty goal with the final kick of this enthralling encounter broke Ospreys hearts, and condemned us to yet another defeat, thus denting our play-off hopes. All however is not lost as other teams in the Magners League could well do us a favour.

We managed to outscore Munster by two tries to one but once again suffered for our indiscipline as O'Gara racked up seventeen points. In the first quarter Munster came close to scoring when Lifeimi Mafi's searing break released Keith Earls on the left wing. His delicate chip ahead resulted in a race between Tommy Bowe, Richard Fussell and the Munsterman, but Fussell's desperate tackle saved the day as Earls knocked on. We counteracted in fine style and it seemed curtains for the visitors as Fussell and Hibbard freed James Hook, but a magnificent last-ditch tackle by scrum-half Conor Murray forced the centre three-quarter into touch.

Eventually, replacement David Wallace crossed for the first try of the evening, thanks to a forage

Ronan O'Gara kicks Munster to victory at the Liberty.

from the combative Damien Hurley. But we responded in fine style at the start of the second half as I was driven over the try line after a typical Ospreys maul. We were now in the ascendancy and when referee Garces awarded us a penalty try for persistent collapsing of the scrummage, it seemed the writing was on the wall. However, O'Gara's pinpoint accuracy kept Munster in the match and when an over-eager defence was penalised for offside whilst charging his drop-goal attempt, we knew we were beaten.

What a disappointing final home appearance for Lee Byrne who was replaced after thirty minutes as he limped off the field.

Ospreys: Byrne, Walker, Bowe, Hook, Fussell, Biggar, Webb, Bevington, Hibbard, A Jones, Gough, AW Jones (c), Tipuric, Thomas, Holah	Munster: F Jones, Howlett, Mafi, Warwick, Earls, O'Gara (c), Murray, Horan, Varley, Hayes, Nagle, O'Callaghan, Ryan, Wallace, Coughlan
Replacements: Bennett, P James, D Jones, R Jones, Collins, Phillips, Bishop, Parker	Replacements: Sherry, du Preez, Buckley, O'Donnell, Ronan, Stringer, Barnes, Zebo
Ospreys 20 AW Jones (t), penalty try, Biggar (2c, 1pg), Hook (1pg)	
Munster 22 Wallace (t), O'Gara (5pg, 1c)	
Referee: Jerome Garces FFR	**Attendance:** 10,247

May 6

Aironi v Ospreys (*Magners*, Stadio Luigi Zaffanella, Viadana)

Coach Sean Holley summed up our feelings at the end of another sub-standard performance: 'We're disappointed with our display and we're disappointed with our form since the Six Nations.' There was nothing more to be said as players and management honestly conceded shortcomings to the press after the match. However, the Scarlets' convincing win over the Cardiff Blues meant that we would be competing in a play-off semi-final against Munster at Thomond Park in a week's time.

We certainly left it late – a James Hook penalty goal with 75 minutes on the clock clinched the victory. I honestly thought the win was deserved as we were the team intent on playing rugby. However, Aironi's defence and enthusiasm was first class and credit must be given to Rowland Phillips and his coaching team who have certainly worked hard to mould the Italians into a solid outfit.

It is often said that good sides claim the points even when they malfunction, and it was true of the Ospreys on this occasion.

Aironi: Horacio San Martin, Pratichetti, Pavan, Pizarro, Demas, Marshall, Tebaldi (Canavosio 72), Alberto de Marchi (Andrea de Marchi 75), Ferraro (Ongaro 40), Staibano (Redolfini 71), Bortolami (Biagi 78), Geldenhuys, Furno, Sole, Krause (Cattina 42)	Ospreys: Fussell, Bowe, Bishop (Beck 48), Hook, Walker, Biggar (Isaac 60), Webb (Parker (70), James (Bevington (50'), Hibbard, A Jones, R Jones, AW Jones (capt), Tipuric (Smith 74), Thomas, Holah (Gough 60')
Not used: Toniolatti, Bocchino	Not used: Bennett, D Jones,
Aironi 10 Demas (t), Tebaldi (1c, 1pg)	
Ospreys 12 Biggar (3pg), Hook (1pg)	
Referee: Andy MacPherson (SRFU)	**Attendance:** 3,700

May 14

Munster v Ospreys (Magners League semi-final, Thomond Park, Limerick)

At the end of a rollercoaster season, during which we had been magnificent and mediocre in equal measure, would we be up for it? Would the season end in a climax or a catastrophe? Would the Ospreys fizzle and fire, or would we lamely succumb to the Munster juggernaut? These were questions which I just wasn't able to answer as the aeroplane soared skywards towards Shannon Airport.

The first hour was controlled by Munster who never wavered in their determination to reach the Magners League final and win some more silverware in a cabinet which seems to stretch from Limerick to Cork. We had our opportunities, determinedly kept in touch but failed to take advantage of scoring opportunities when they materialised. With a spirited team display at the end taking the match clock well past 80 minutes, there were no tears at the final whistle – we had to accept that Munster were the better side on the day even if the scoreboard testified to a close encounter.

Munster: Felix Jones, Howlett, Barnes (Zebo 74), Mafi, Earls, O'Gara, Murray (Stringer 56), M Horan (du Preez 56), Varley (Sherry 56), Hayes (Archer 62), O'Callaghan, O'Connell (c), Ryan, Coughlan (Leamy 61, Ronan 74), Wallace	**Ospreys:** Fussell, Bowe, Bishop, Hook (Beck 39), Walker, Biggar, Webb (Isaacs 54), James, Bennett (Hibbard 48), A Jones (Griffiths 72), Gough (Collins 48), AW Jones (c), R Jones (Holah 64), Thomas, Tipuric (Smith 74)
Not used: Paul Warwick	Not used: Ryan Bevington
Munster 18: Barnes (2t), O'Gara (2pg, 1c)	
Ospreys 11: Fussell (t), Biggar (2pg)	
Referee: N Owens (Wales)	**Attendance:** 21,217

Fond farewells. Like so many others, these fans are sorry to see James Hook go.

'On the shoulders of giants . . .'
Adam Jones and Ryan Jones (far right)
help me to see further against Munster,
as Rhys Webb (far left) waits for possession.

'My ball!'
Tommy Bowe and Munster's Keith
Earls try to claim possession.

'On your own head be it.'
Munster's All Black winger Doug Howlett gets
a worm-eye's view of Ryan Jones's studs, with
Richard Fussell in attendance.

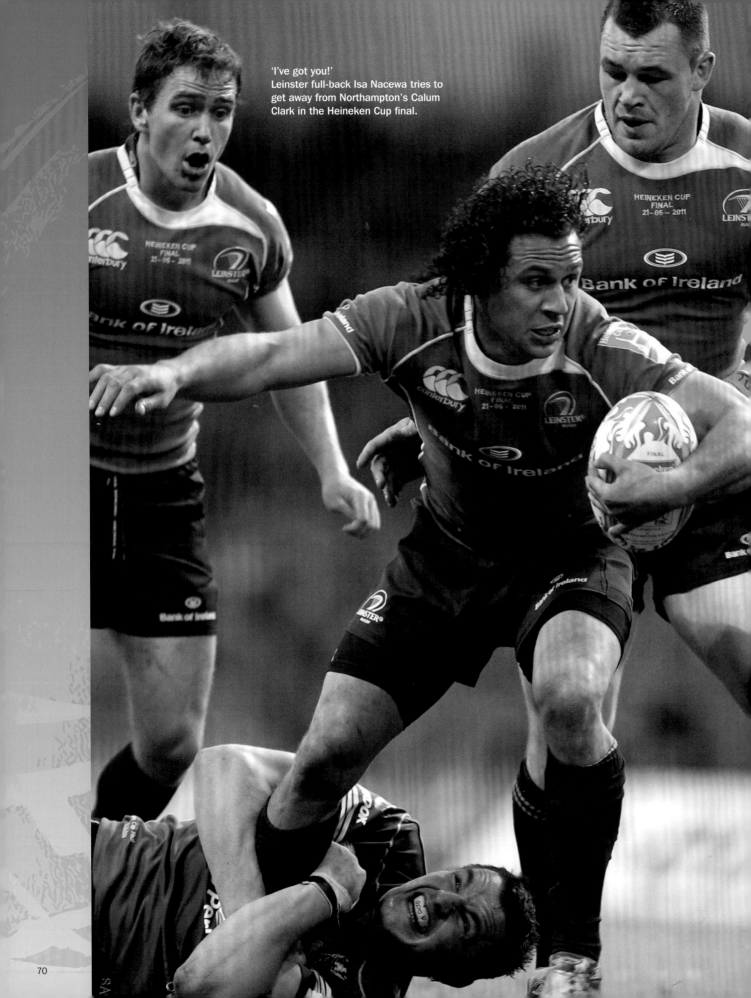

'I've got you!'
Leinster full-back Isa Nacewa tries to get away from Northampton's Calum Clark in the Heineken Cup final.

Two Finals: What a Finish!

May 6

Leinster v Northampton (Heineken Cup Final, Millennium Stadium)

It certainly was a great day out. It would have been the perfect day if the Ospreys had been involved in a Heineken final at Cardiff, but that dream disappeared at the Madejski Stadium in late January. However, an invitation from Adidas to attend the grand final and to witness proceedings from the comfort of their hospitality box was immediately accepted and I looked forward immensely to a few drinks, a tasty meal and a mouth-watering contest between two of Europe's most consistent teams during season 2010/11. Northampton had defeated all opposition and their demolition of Perpignan in the semi-final had possibly made them slight favourites with the pundits. However, I sided with Leinster. I suppose that playing against them on a regular basis gave me a slight advantage as I was well aware of their strengths, and that their weaknesses could be listed on the back of a first-class stamp.

It was a classical confrontation involving the greatest comeback in Heineken Cup history. Leinster were totally despondent at half-time and some supporters must have been checking early evening return flights to Dublin. They had been demolished by a Northampton XV who could do nothing wrong. Dylan Hartley's team had the Midas touch, and everyone present, from the supporters to match stewards, felt that the cup was already theirs.

However, Leinster reappeared in determined mood. Apparently young Jonny Sexton had reminded his squad of what Liverpool had achieved in the 2006 Champions League Final when the Merseysiders had fought back heroically from a 3–0 deficit to claim the spoils in Istanbul against AC Milan. Within minutes of the restart Leinster were back in the game with Sexton inspirational in the mother of all comebacks.

Man of the Match Jonny Sexton with the Heineken Cup.

It was a magnificent match with Leo Cullen's side proving once again that the game is never over until the final whistle. Man of the match Jonny Sexton became only the third player, after Sebastien Carrat (Brive v Leicester 1997) and Leon Lloyd (Leiester v Stade Français 2001), to score two tries in a Heineken Cup final. It was an incredible day out . . . but next year I desperately want to be out there as a participant!

Leinster: Nacewa, Horgan, O'Driscoll, D'Arcy (McFadden 67'), Fitzgerald, Sexton (Madigan 78'), Reddan (Boss 72'), Healy (van der Merwe 58'), Strauss (Harris-Wright 79'), Ross (Wright 78'), Cullen (c), Hines (Toner 78'), McLaughlin (Jennings 41'), Heaslip, O'Brien

Northampton: Foden, Ashton (Commins 78'), Clarke (Mercey 27'-37', Mujati 66'), Downey (Ansbro 66'), Diggin, Myler (Geraghty 66'), Dickson, Tonga'uiha (Waller 66'), Hartley (c) (Sharman 69'), Mujati (Mercey 66'), Lawes, Day (Sorenson 78'), Clark, Wilson (Easter 63'), Dowson.

Leinster 33 Sexton (2t, 3c, 4pg) Hines (t)

Northampton 22 Dowson (t), Foden (t), Hartley (t), Myler (2c, 1pg)

Referee: Romain Poite (FFR)   **Attendance:** 72,456

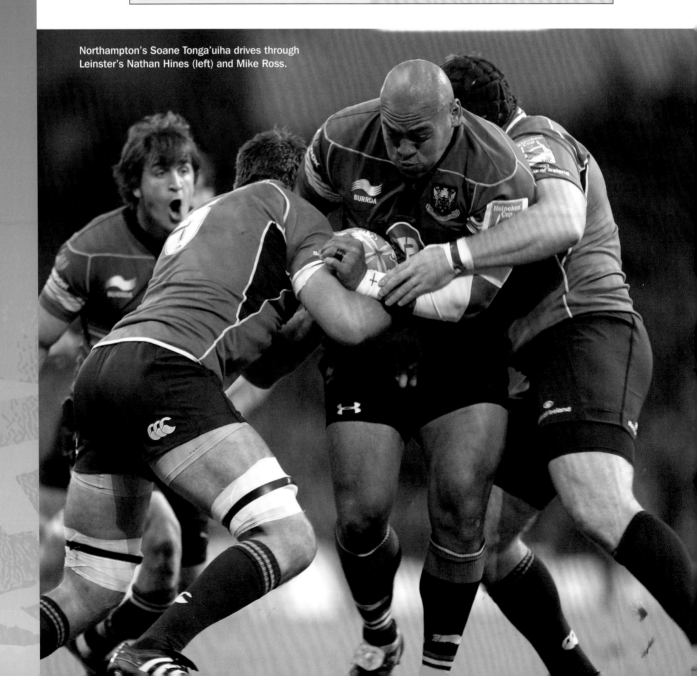

Northampton's Soane Tonga'uiha drives through Leinster's Nathan Hines (left) and Mike Ross.

'In BOD we trust.'
Brian O'Driscoll in Leinster colours.

Saturday, May 28

From THE BEVAN BULLETIN

Leinster v Munster

(Magners League Final,
Thomond Park, Limerick)

One had the feeling that Munster wanted it more. The Heineken Cup winners' dream of a double were shattered by arch-rivals Munster who totally outplayed the city slickers with a totally committed performance throughout. Coach Tony McGahan had called for an all-out display and that's exactly what he got! Leinster retaliated strongly at the start of the second half but Munster sealed the win when O'Gara hoisted a cross kick which was taken by Earls who avoided Nacewa's lunge and scored despite a last ditch tackle from Shane Horgan. It really was a magnificent season for the Irish provinces – Leinster winning the Heineken Cup, Munster crowned Magners League champions, Ulster's resurgence resulting in encouraging performances in all competitions, and Connacht qualifying for next season's Heineken Cup for the very first time.

Leinster: Nacewa, Horgan, O'Driscoll, McFadden, Fitzgerald, Sexton, Reddan (O'Donohoe 77'), van der Merwe (Healy 60'), Strauss (Dundon 70'), Ross (Wright 68'), Cullen (c), Hines, O'Brien (McLaughlin 60'), Heaslip, Jennings
Not used: Toner, Madigan, O'Malley

Munster: Jones (Warwick 75'), Howlett, Barnes, Mafi, Earls, O'Gara, Murray, Horan (du Preez 53'), Varley (Sherry 59'), Hayes, O'Callaghan (Leamy 68'), O'Connell (c), Ryan, Coughlan, Wallace
Not used: Archer, Ronan, Stringer, Murphy

Munster 19 penalty try, Howlett (t), Earls (t), O'Gara (2 c)

Leinster 9 Sexton (3 pg)

Referee: Nigel Owens (WRU)

Attendance: 26,100

Swansea City manager Brendan Rogers takes
victory over Nottingham Forest in his stride . . .

CHAPTER 9

Swans Flying High

May 16

Swansea City v Nottingham Forest (Championship Play-off Semi-final, Liberty Stadium)

I was there! Tickets were at a premium but, along with several other Ospreys, I was present for that nail-biting win. I'm sure I speak for my team-mates in saying we thoroughly enjoyed being part of a great occasion for the club and the city of Swansea.

The Swans were firm favourites to reach the Wembley play-off final after a tenacious display against Forest at the City Ground the previous Thursday evening. The scoreless draw was a remarkable achievement considering Neil Taylor had been sent off after just 38 seconds. Before the teams appeared, the announcer reminded the crowd that it was a year to the day since Besian Idrizaj, the young striker signed from Liverpool, died from heart failure. The team dedicated the season to his memory and he would have been proud of their performances.

In the 28th minute Swansea conjured a goal which could have graced the Nou Camp, as Britton turned athletically to shoot into the far corner. Five minutes later Dobbie mesmerised the defence allowing him the time and space to glide the ball into an unguarded net. It was total football and testimony to the play witnessed at the Stadium throughout the season.

The second half was tight, but with ten minutes to go the diminutive Welshman Rob Earnshaw appeared for Forest and scored immediately. Minutes later the former Cardiff City striker came within a whisker of doubling his tally. But Swansea held their nerve and added a third goal when Darren Pratley broke free and coolly swept the ball goalwards. Wembley – and the Premier League – here we come!

Swansea City: de Vries, Rangel, Monk (c), Williams, Tate; Britton, Allen (Moore 84'), Dobbie (Pratley 59'); Dyer, Borini, Sinclair (Serran 88')	**Nottingham Forest:** Camp (c); Moloney, Chambers, Morgan, Gunter; McGugan, Moussi, McGoldrick (Earnshaw 77'); Tyson (Majewski 62'), Tiudgay (Boyd 67')
Swansea City **3** Britton, Dobbie, Pratley (2)	
Nottingham Forest 1 Earnshaw	
Referee: A Marriner (West Midlands)	**Attendance:** 19,816

Joe Allen of Swansea City takes on Lewis McGugan of Nottingham Forest.

Magners main man. Cardiff Blues centre Casey Laulala tries to step out of another tackle.

Dream Teams

Now let me say at the very outset that I'm not a great believer in Dream XVs, teams of the season and outfits selected to represent Planet Earth against constellations in distant orbits.

But if you're actually selected for one of these teams, things change, don't they? And as I've been included in *Rugby World*'s Magners Team of the Season, it would be ungracious to knock it! And to play against us I've also included Will Greenwood's Aviva Premiership team of the season as printed in *The Daily Telegraph* on Friday, May 13, 2011.

Magners XV		Aviva Premiership XV
Isa Nacewa	15	Ben Foden
Fion Carr	14	Chris Ashton
Casey Laulala	13	Seru Rabeni
Jonathan Davies	12	Brad Barritt
Tim Visser	11	Joe Maddock
Ronan O'Gara	10	Toby Flood
Ruan Pienaar	9	Ben Youngs
Iestyn Thomas	1	Soane Tonga'uiha
Richardt Strauss	2	Schalk Brits
Mike Ross	3	Dan Cole
Alun Wyn Jones	4	Juandre Kruger
Richie Gray	5	Geoff Parling
Sean O'Brien	6	Phil Dowson
Jamie Heaslip	8	Ernst Joubert
Sam Warburton	7	Steffon Armitage

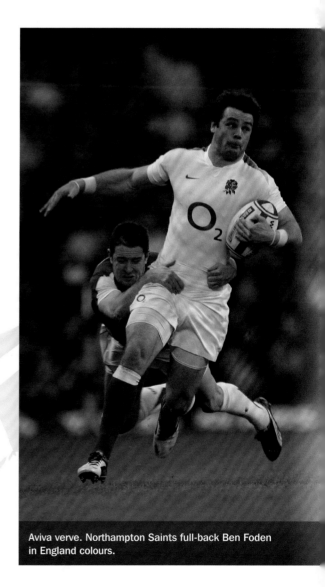

Aviva verve. Northampton Saints full-back Ben Foden in England colours.

I think I'm starting to develop a fondness for these dream teams after all, so I'm including one of my own, based on those Six Nations players that Wales played against this season.

Alun Wyn Jones's Six Nations Team of the Season 2010/2011

15   **Andrea Masi (Racing Metro 92 and Italy)**

14   **Tommy Bowe (Ospreys and Ireland)**
13   **Brian O'Driscoll (Leinster and Ireland)**
12   **Sean Lamont (Scarlets and Scotland)**
11   **Chris Ashton (Northampton and England)**

10   **Toby Flood (Leicester and England)**
9   **Morgan Parra (ASM Clermont Auvergne and France)**

1   **Thomas Domingo (ASM Clermont Auvergne and France)**
2   **Dylan Hartley (Northampton and England)**
3   **Martin Castrogiovanni (Leicester and Italy)**

4   **Richie Gray (Glasgow Warriors and Scotland)**
5   **Paul O'Connell (Munster and Ireland)**

6   **Sean O'Brien (Leinster and Ireland)**
8   **Sergio Parisse (Stade Français and Italy)**
7   **Imanol Harinordoquy (Biarritz Olympique Pays Basque and France)**

The best number eight in Europe, France's Imanol Harinordoquy, in my side at number seven.

The other best number eight in Europe, Italy's Sergio Parisse!

Richie Gray

Martin Castrogiovanni

Stephen Jones –
'A great player, a great ambassador and a great guy.'

A Gentleman amongst Barbarians

June 4

Wales v Barbarians (Millennium Stadium)

Playing alongside Stephen Jones has been an honour and privilege. He deserves his hundred caps, as he is a great player, a great ambassador and a great guy. Pity we couldn't manufacture a win to celebrate his huge achievement.

It certainly was a grand occasion, however, and we failed only by the narrowest of margins. The Barbarians secured possession in the dying seconds and with a length-of-the-field movement crossed for a match-winning try. Although it was billed as an international, Wales entered into the spirit of the contest and attacked from everywhere, and in true Barbarian fashion refused all kicks at goal.

The main purpose of the afternoon was to blood new players and kick off preparations for Rugby World Cup 2011. Stephen's hundredth international, Gavin's return, in addition to the selection of a star-studded Barbarian squad, ensured there was a respectable crowd who were treated to a feast of rugby. It has to be said that the final try was an outstanding effort with that man Nacewa again proving himself at the highest level. What an incredible season he's had.

We'll have to wait and see whether he represents Fiji at this year's Rugby World Cup. He appeared as a late substitute for his country of birth at Rugby World Cup 2007 but then decided he wanted to play for New Zealand. His dispute with the IRB has been an on-going affair but it seems his one appearance for Fiji means his options are limited.

Wales: Stoddart, North, J Davies, Henson, A Brew, S Jones, M Phillips, Bevington, Bennett, P James, R Jones, Charteris, Lydiate, Faletau, Warburton (c.)
Replacements: Burns, Andrews, AW Jones, Turnbull, Knoyle, Priestland, Scott Williams
Sin Bin: A Brew (44')

Barbarians: Nacewa (Leinster and Fiji), Sackey (Toulon and England), Rabeni (La Rochelle and Fiji), Bastareaud (Stade Francais Paris and France), Howlett (Munster and New Zealand), James (Clermont Auvergne), Tillous-Borde (Castres Olympique and France), Thomas (Scarlets and Wales), Bruno (Toulon and France), Hayman (Toulon and New Zealand), Tekori (Castres Olympique and Samoa), Tito (Cardiff Blues), van Niekerk (Toulon and South Africa), Parisse (c Stade Francais Paris and Italy), Williams (Cardiff Blues and Wales)
Replacements: Ghiraldini (Benetton Treviso and Italy), Kubriashvili (Toulon and Georgia), Lund (Biarritz Olympique and Norway), Smith (Toulon and Australia), Williams (Cardiff Blues), Mason (Toulon), Baby (Clermont Auvergne and France)
Sin Bin: Tekori (45')

Wales **28** North (t), Stoddart (t), Phillips (t), Brew (t), Jones (4c)

Barbarians 31 Tekori (t), Nacewa (2t), Parisse (t), Bastareaud (t), B James (3c)

Referee: Alain Rolland (IRL) **Attendance:** 48,632

100 caps for a 100 percenter. Stephen Jones leads Wales on to the field against the Barbarians at Cardiff.

Try time! George North takes All Black legend Doug Howlett over the line with him.

Isa-metrics! Full-back Isa Nacewa escapes the clutches of Toby Faletau, leaving Morgan Stoddart, Tavis Knoyle and George North at contrasting degrees of resignation.

Scarlets, Wales and British Lions hooker Matthew Rees. Though named as Wales's World Cup summer training squad captain, injury would deny him a trip to New Zealand in the autumn.

JUNE

In the mix

June 6

Wales's World Cup summer training squad announced:

Lee Byrne (Clermont Auvergne), Mike Phillips (Bayonne), James Hook (Perpignan), Gavin Henson (unattached), Dwayne Peel (Sale Sharks), Leigh Halfpenny, Jamie Roberts, Richie Rees, Lloyd Williams (Blues), Aled Brew, Jason Tovey (Dragons), Andrew Bishop, Shane Williams (Ospreys), George North, Jonathan Davies, Morgan Stoddart, Scott Williams, Stephen Jones, Rhys Priestland, Tavis Knoyle (Scarlets); Andy Powell (Sale Sharks), Gareth Delve (Melbourne Rebels), Craig Mitchell (Exeter Chiefs), Scott Andrews, Gethin Jenkins, John Yapp, Bradley Davies, Sam Warburton, Martyn Williams (Blues), Lloyd Burns, Luke Charteris, Toby Faletau, Dan Lydiate (Dragons), Adam Jones, Ryan Bevington, Huw Bennett, Paul James, Alun Wyn Jones, Ryan Jones, Justin Tipuric, Jonathan Thomas (Ospreys), Matthew Rees (c), Ken Owens, Josh Turnbull, Lou Reed, Rob McCusker (Scarlets).

Alun Wyn Bevan: Tell me Alun, how stressed are you prior to a squad announcement?

Alun Wyn Jones: Twenty caps, fifty caps, a hundred caps . . . you still feel uneasy. Every professional sportsman in a team game desperately wants to receive confirmation of their inclusion. These days it's either by hearing your name on radio or television, reading about it in the national or local press or via text messages or e-mails. No one takes anything for granted . . . your last cap could be your final one!

AWB: The players named will have to impress the coaches during the summer months on the field of play and the training paddock, and in the weights room and gymnasium. Then from an initial list of over forty players, the coach Warren Gatland will reach for his guillotine and eventually announce thirty names a few weeks prior to departure. Obviously, you won't be taking anything for granted.

AWJ: I've been given this opportunity and intend focusing intensely to ensure that I'm prepared physically and mentally for the challenge. Everything else will be on the back-burner. The warm-up games – two against England and one against Argentina – are crucial to our preparations. We fully intend qualifying from our group and gaining the respect which could see us progress to the final stages of the competition. Let's remember, Wales reached the semi-finals when the competition was staged in Australia and New Zealand in 1987, and also shocked the rugby world when they nearly beat the eventual champions England in 2003. There's always a surprise package in Rugby World Cups . . . Argentina shocked us all in 2007.

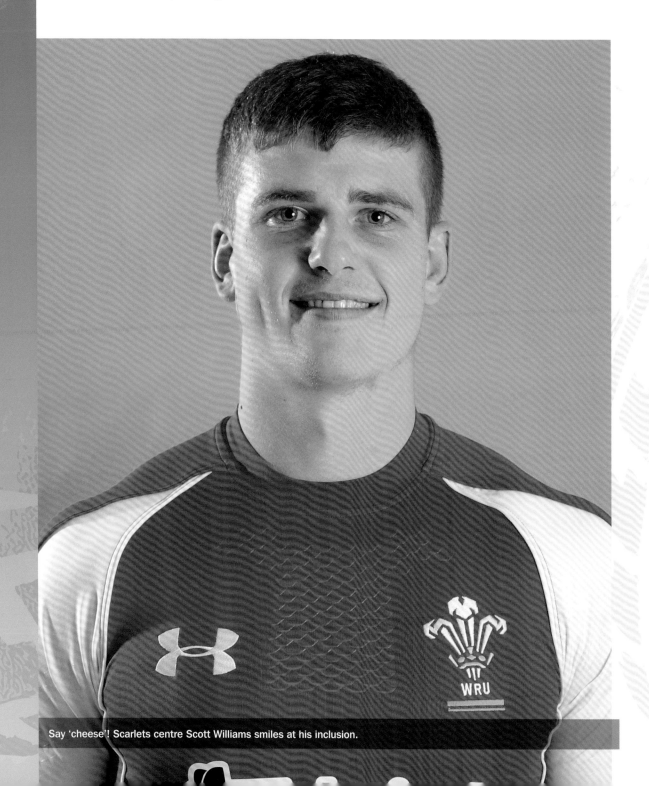

Say 'cheese'! Scarlets centre Scott Williams smiles at his inclusion.

'Hair we go, hair we go, hair we go!'
Dragons number eight Toby Faletau,
one of a number of exciting young back
rowers in the squad.

A day out. Sitting outside Aberaeron's Harbourmaster hotel, where S4C's drama series *Teulu* was being filmed at the time, hence the temporary 'Pen y Cei' sign. (pic. Phill Davies)

The Original Ospreys

The first week in June 2011 was of immense importance to ornithologists the world over. For the first time since 1604, osprey chicks successfully hatched near the Dyfi estuary in Cardiganshire. It was quite a coincidence that we'd decided to pay a visit to the area in the very week that the Dyfi Osprey Project had been national headline material.

If I'm honest, I've always been more naturist than naturalist; the beaches of Copacabana, Cannes and Caswell have always proved more alluring than birds' nests. So I remained to be convinced that this particular visit to mid-Wales would be much of an addition to our almanac. Then again, there was a certain witty symmetry in the idea of the Ospreys rugby captain popping in and saying hello to his avian counterpart!

Before the visit, several internet search engines helped me learn more about this extraordinary bird. Its eyesight is apparently six times as powerful as man's (no dropping vital passes for this creature!), and it is the only bird on earth which feeds exclusively on fish. And I was to learn more from the knowledgeable staff at the project's headquarters. Whilst the power produced by the osprey's legs and wings is quite remarkable, they stressed that surprise is the bird's ultimate weapon as it crash dives devastatingly with its talons hurled forward for the expected cull. I soon realised that my Ospreys could benefit from this bird's philosophy!

Emyr, Elwyn and Mair were the ideal hosts as we became acquainted with the ospreys' habits and lifestyle. They were so enthusiastic about the species, and the visitors were treated to a wildlife spectacular in the appropriate hides where live pictures were transmitted. I have to admit that I was glued to the plasma screens and couldn't quite come to terms with the size of the bird and the dimension of the nest which must have been as big as a king-size bed!

The three chicks, which we could see on the live feed from the nest, require constant feeding and, whilst the parents have no difficulty in catching fish in good weather, it has to be said that the sun doesn't always shine in Wales. Visibility deteriorated during our visit and from the hide, through a pair of powerful binoculars, I could see the male sitting tight until the rain abated.

I spy with my little eye . . . Osprey-spotting on the Dyfi, under Elwyn's watchful eye. (pic. Alun Wyn Bevan)

Before leaving, the site's Warden Emyr Evans, reminded me that the birds had at one time been regular visitors to the Swansea area. I was aware of this fact as the osprey is featured on Swansea's coat of arms. Who knows they might just well return in the near future and inspire their namesakes to greater things!

The visit over, it was now time for lunch. Our chosen port of call was the Georgian town of Aberaeron on the Cardiganshire coast where we had booked a table at the Harbourmaster, and where the food was delicious and served in great surroundings with friendly staff. A weekend in Aberaeron was becoming more and more appealing, but it was time to head home. I recognise that I have a certain affinity with Cardiganshire, my *taid* having taught in the County School at Cardigan and my mother was actually born and brought up in the town. There is a sense of tranquillity that sits over the area that is a million miles away from the hustle and bustle that I grew up with in Swansea.

With the man who knows his birds, RSPB warden Emyr Evans. (pic. Alun Wyn Bevan)

There's no wriggling out of this tackle. An osprey in its element.

(pic. Andy Rouse)

A word to the wise.
Wales coach Warren
Gatland takes me to
one side.

JULY

Flight to Warsaw

July 1

AWB: In preparation for the World Cup, the Welsh rugby squad is about to embark upon its summer training camp – in Poland! Isn't there a concern that the Welsh rugby team will be recognised as being highly tuned and nutritionally prepared for Rugby World Cup 2011 but might be found wanting when it comes to carrying that oval ball over the goal line? What benefits can truly be derived from spending periods in a refrigerator?

AWJ: As players, we will be experiencing totally alien conditions in Poland. From a comfort point of view we'd all prefer to be spending time in luxurious surroundings in training camps such as Club La Santa in Lanzarote. However, we're not going to excel at this year's RWC by lounging on a deck chair or by being pampered in five-star hotels!

We will be spending time in an ice chamber in the middle of Poland. We'll be based at the Olympic training facility in Spala undergoing temperatures as low as minus 150 degrees centigrade wearing nothing but swimming trunks and special gloves and stockings to cover up our extremities and guard against frostbite. We'll also be wearing masks which will help us to breathe normally because the air in the chamber is too cold to inhale. We are used to cold treatments. All of us at one time or another have plunged into ice baths which help recovery, but the chambers in Spala will be completely different.

The whole point of the visit is to produce a prolonged and intense training programme, as well as aiding recovery from injury. It should benefit Leigh Halfpenny, Shane Williams, Gethin Jenkins and Lee Byrne. Our physical performance coaches have explained that the chambers at Spala enable players to train longer, harder and more often. I hope I've answered both questions – we are actually looking forward to the visit and accept, though it isn't going to be easy, that the benefits can most definitely be substantial. Good performances on the rugby field are all about good preparation and if we're all physically and mentally prepared, we will be better equipped for the forthcoming match roster.

A veteran – at 25 years old! Leading Wales out at Twickenham for my fiftieth cap.

AUGUST

From the fridge to the warm-up

August 6

England v Wales (Twickenham)

It was my 50th cap and a proud occasion for myself and the family. Although the result favoured England, it was a performance which brought a smile to our faces. England's forwards were dominant in the first fifty minutes and allowed Jonny Wilkinson time and space to control play. Defensively Wales were superb and everyone in the post-match frenzy paid tribute to our resilience. When Tuilagi crossed for the home side's second try early in the second half, the chariot seemed unstoppable. However, with half an hour remaining, Wales took a stranglehold on the match with George North and Shane Williams crossing for two late tries. I have no hesitation in saying that we would have won the match had there been five more minutes remaining on the clock. England seemed shell shocked at the final whistle, whilst Wales produced a performance which can only bolster confidence prior to the return fixture and the Rugby World Cup.

We were all highly delighted with the performance of Rhys Priestland who was thrust into the spotlight just minutes prior to kick-off when Stephen Jones pulled out with a calf strain. He showed uncanny judgement and proved to all concerned that he is a quality footballer. His Scarlets team-mate Morgan Stoddart suffered a broken leg in a fairly innocuous tackle and one can only praise the Sky TV producer for not replaying the incident on television. The incident brought back memories of Aaron Ramsey's injury playing for Arsenal against Stoke in February 2010. Nice of Aaron to twitter, 'Hope Morgan has a speedy recovery.'

England: Armitage, Banahan, Tuilagi (Sharples 59'), Flutey, Cueto, Wilkinson (Hodgson 76'), Care (Wigglesworth 58'), Corbisiero (Stevens 71'), Hartley (Mears 58'), Stevens (Wilson 58'), Shaw (Botha 58'), Palmer, Croft, Haskell, Moody (c) (Wood 60')	Wales: Stoddart (Scott Williams 48'), North, J Davies, Roberts, Shane Williams, Priestland, Phillips (Knoyle 61'), James (Bevington 65'), Bennett (Burns 65'), Mitchell, B Davies, AW Jones (Charteris 65'), Lydiate, Faletau (R Jones 55'), Warburton (c)
England 23 Haskell (t), Tuilagi (t), Wilkinson (1pg, 2dg, 2c)	
Wales 19 North (2t), Shane Williams (t), Priestland (2c)	
Referee: Steve Walsh (ARU)	**Attendance:** 80,945

Two-try scorer George North has eyes only for the ball despite Mark Cueto's challenge.

Morgan Stoddart's broken leg at Twickenham rules him out of the World Cup.

Rhys Priestland steps inside Toby Flood at Cardiff. Rhys would later prove one of Wales's great successes at the World Cup.

August 13

Wales v England

(Millennium Stadium)

We applied ourselves. We stuck at it. We never wavered in our determination and belief, and achieved a remarkable victory.

In all sports one must take advantage of opportunities when they arise and England were guilty of schoolboy errors in a first half which they dominated. What were they thinking of when they spurned several goal-kicking chances? It has to be said that our defence in that one-sided first half was absolutely outstanding and the scoreboard confirmed that we were still in the hunt.

It proved, for the second time in a fortnight, to be a game of two halves. We eventually managed some excellent possession, our back row foraged ferociously allowing our three-quarters to attack with creativity and pace. We were sharper and more incisive than our one-dimensional opponents. And just as at Twickenham, we held the upper hand psychologically, as well as physically, in the final quarter. James Hook's try was the final nail in the coffin. The win might have surprised the critics but with fifteen minutes remaining the players were quietly confident. Home and away results are taken into consideration in Champions League encounters – we'd outscored England in terms of aggregate scores and try count! Marvellous!

A Welsh All Black! Full-back James Hook scores the game's only try as England's James Haskell arrives too late.

Wales: Hook, North, Roberts, Henson (Scott Williams 32'), Shane Williams, Priestland (Brew 41'), Phillips, James (Bevington 61'), Burns (Bennett 53'), Mitchell (James 77'), Charteris, AW Jones (Turnbull 60'), Lydiate, Faletau, Warburton(c)
Yellow card: Roberts (41), Phillips (71)

England: Foden, Banahan, Tindall(c) (Armitage 59', Tindall back on 74'), Hape, Cueto, Flood (Hodgson 68'), Wigglesworth (Care 30'), Corbisiero (Stevens 59'), Thompson (Mears 59'), Cole, Deacon (Palmer 68'), Lawes, Wood, Easter, Fourie (Haskell 50')

Wales 19 Hook (t, c, 2pg); Priestland (2pg)

England 9 Flood (3pg)

Referee: A Rolland (IRFU)

Attendance: 73,000

Front and back page pin-up. Gavin Henson, in form against England, but injured after half an hour, would later lose his fitness battle for the World Cup.

August 16

It was with a great deal of sadness that everyone in Wales learnt of the untimely death of Huw Ceredig. Huw had made his name as the pub landlord Reg Harries in the S4C soap opera *Pobol y Cwm*. Non-Welsh speakers had come to love him as the character Fatty Lewis in the film *Twin Town*. As one who has grown up in Swansea, I never tire of watching what has now become a cult movie.

What is interesting to note is the reception the film receives on first viewing from our Southern Hemisphere players. We watch it regularly on away trips. They just don't get the humour, but after a couple of months in Swansea the penny drops and they are rolling about like the rest of us.

Huw was an all-round sports fanatic and a huge fan of George Best. There is a story told about the night he called in at the Heronston Hotel on the Ewenny Road in Bridgend because he had heard that George was there doing a book signing. On spotting Huw in the queue, the Manchester United superstar rushed towards him and enveloped him in a warm embrace. He'd also enjoyed *Twin Town*!

August 20

Wales v Argentina (Millennium Stadium)

The first 37 minutes belonged to the visitors who were disciplined, well organised and threatened on more than one occasion to create try-scoring opportunities. However, just before the interval we delivered two knockout punches. Firstly, Tavis Knoyle, having received the ball from Andy Powell, broke through finding me in support, and my inside pass released Andy who sprinted 30 metres for his first international try. We then crossed for a second try directly from the restart which was won by Bradley Davies. From the ensuing ruck we counter-attacked from our own 22 with Tavis Knoyle and Jamie Roberts distributing swiftly to the powerful George North. He in turn beat two defenders with pace and guile, and whilst he could have gone for the corner he unselfishly passed inside to me! James Hook succeeded with both conversions and when we departed for the dressing rooms at half-time we were 14–3 ahead.

Scrum-half Tavis Knoyle takes on Argentina's Juan Martin Fernandez-Lobbe, with George North (left) in support.

Looking back objectively at the match, I have to admit that we were under the cosh in the line-out. If we can become a little more efficient in that area we will be able to exert more pressure with the possession we have. On occasions we are a bit over zealous at the line. However, there are many positives to be gained from the preparatory matches.

We've become an 80-minute side; the work put in over the summer means that we are physically better equipped than we have been in the past. Statistically, the five victories in our last seven matches has given us a psychological boost prior to the sport's ultimate challenge, the Rugby World Cup.

The second half proved a rather drab affair with further James Hook penalties and a well-created George North try ensuring a comfortable victory. One of three former Llandovery College schoolboys in the squad (Andy Powell and I are the others), George has become quite an influential player and his strike rate of six touchdowns in eight matches makes him a player of real quality.

'Well done, old boy!' Fellow scorer (and ex-Llandovery College pupil) Andy Powell congratulates me heartily on my try. I, on the other hand, look quite sick!

Wales: Byrne (Brew 57'), Halfpenny, J Davies, Roberts (Scott Williams 66'), North, Hook, Knoyle (Ll Williams 61'), James, Hibbard (Bennett 66'), Adam Jones (Bevington 62'), AW Jones, B Davies, Lydiate (Thomas 57'), Powell, M Williams (c) (Tipuric 61')	**Argentina:** Rodriguez, Agulla (Imhoff 57'), Bosch, Fernandez, Camacho, Contepomi (c), Vergallo, Ronciero (Figallo 67'), Ledesma (Creevy 51'), Figallo (Scelzo 40'), Carizza (Gallarza 69'), Albacete, Cabello, JM Fernandez-Lobbe, Leguizamon (Campos 65') Yellow card : JM Fernandez-Lobbe (54')

Wales   28 Powell (t), AW Jones (t), North (t), Hook (2c, 3pg)

Argentina 13 Scelzo (t), Contepomi (1c, 2pg)

Referee: Romain Poite (FFR)	**Attendance:** 51,951

Don't slice, don't hook. Another kick going straight between the uprights for fly half James Hook against Argentina.

Because they're there . . .
The heroic Richard Parks.

On Top of the World

One of the most special of special guests at the Millennium Stadium when Wales played England on August 13 was Richard Parks, the former Pontypridd, Celtic Warriors, Leeds, Perpignan, Newport Gwent Dragons and Wales open-side wing-forward.

On July 12 he had become the first ever person to climb the highest summits on each of the world's continents and stand on all three poles (the North Pole, the South Pole and the summit of Everest). He completed his challenge on the top of Mount Erebus, Europe's highest peak, in six months, 11 days, seven hours and 53 minutes.

He had been given a spectacular send off at the Millennium Stadium during the 2010 Autumn Internationals before leaving for the South Pole. Prior to his departure to Alaska to scale Mount McKinley (re-named Denali), Richard was also present at the Wales v Barbarians match in June whilst he was recovering from frostbite after his Everest adventure. The Senedd in Cardiff Bay staged a homecoming for Richard in late July and as current players we were delighted to learn that the Welsh Rugby Union had formally invited the former international to the Wales v England fixture as a special guest of WRU President, Dennis Gethin.

As players we all echoed the sentiments expressed by the president – 'Richard's feat will rank as one of the greatest Welsh achievements of all time. He is an inspiration and everyone at the WRU has continued to be impressed by his temarkable feat.' The mountaineer and pioneer is aiming to raise £1 million in aid of Marie Curie Cancer Care and if any readers wish to contribute, they can donate by cheque made payable to '737 Trust' and sent to: 737 Trust, Greystones, 34 Ridgeway, Newport NP20 5AG.

Great effort, great cause.

A farewell to arms? Back-row legend Martyn Williams returns to the dressing room after captaining his country to victory over Argentina. Two days later, he was omitted from the Welsh squad for the World Cup in New Zealand.

CHAPTER 17

World Cup Squad Announced

August 22

At 12 noon at the Vale of Glamorgan campus at Hensol, Warren Gatland released the names of the thirty Welsh players set to travel to New Zealand in early September for the 2011 Rugby World Cup. And there were some surprises. We all felt for Martyn Williams who had given his all over the summer months, and on his 99th international appearance, only 48 hours previously, had captained Wales to victory over Argentina.

My Ospreys colleague Richard Hibbard also missed out as a result of a nasty injury received late on in the Argentina match, whilst the uncapped Ken Owens, who had been released to play for the Scarlets in a friendly against Clermont Auvergne on the weekend, was ecstatic when he was informed of his inclusion. Lee Byrne hardly slept over the weekend – his recent spate of injuries added to a general lack of game time led some critics to question his inclusion in the squad. However, his past reputation proved crucial and on his day he can be a real match-winner. The decision to take five prop forwards was great news for Ryan Bevington who was quite emotional when he took it all in.

Other players who must have been extremely disappointed included back row players Jonathan Thomas, Gareth Delve and Josh Turnbull, scrum-half Dwayne Peel, whilst cruel injuries to Matthew Rees, Gavin Henson and Morgan Stoddart meant that they'd be watching the tournament from the comfort of their homes.

My Ospreys team-mate Richard Hibbard: another to lose out.

Wales at the Rugby World Cup 2011

Back row (l. to r.): Aled Brew (Dragons), Gethin Jenkins (Blues), Adam Jones (Ospreys), Ken Owens (Scarlets), Paul James (Ospreys), Lloyd Burns (Dragons), Ryan Bevington (Ospreys), Tavis Knoyle (Scarlets), Lloyd Williams (Blues), George North (Scarlets), Rhys Priestland (Scarlets)

Middle row: Craig Mitchell (Exeter Chiefs), Jamie Roberts (Blues), Bradley Davies (Blues), Alun Wyn Jones (Ospreys), Luke Charteris (Dragons), Ryan Jones (Ospreys), Andy Powell (Sale Sharks), Toby Faletau (Dragons), Huw Bennett (Ospreys)

Front row: Leigh Halfpenny (Blues), Lee Byrne (Ospreys), Scott Williams (Scarlets), James Hook (Perpignan), Sam Warburton ([c] Blues), Stephen Jones (Scarlets), Mike Phillips (Bayonne), Shane Williams (Ospreys), Jonathan Davies (Scarlets)

Looking the part. Laughing with Gareth Edwards on the banks of the Tywi. Guess which of us is the experienced fisherman?

CHAPTER
18

Tywi Calm before Kiwi Storm

August 26

After a particularly gruelling week of preparations for the Rugby World Cup, the entire squad was eagerly looking forward to Friday, August 26th. We could leave our training base at the Vale of Glamorgan campus for 24 hours and do whatever it was that took our fancy. Most of my fellow squad members chose to just relax, others to play a few rounds of golf while I was off to have lunch with the world's greatest ever rugby player – Gareth Edwards.

This meeting had come about as a result of another casual comment I had let slip to Alun Wyn Bevan about one day wanting to learn the art of fly fishing. And as if by magic Alun had set up a lesson with the great man himself, with Huw Evans (the official WRU photographer) also being on hand to record the event!

The day would begin with lunch at the Polyn, a restaurant situated not far from the Tywi at Nantgaredig. As soon as Gareth arrived, I knew we were in for a wonderful afternoon. He was entertaining, knowledgeable and the conversation flowed easily from one subject to the next. I should add at this point that the food was superb and I would have no problem relating back to our team dietician what I had eaten.

Gareth's choice of main course was obviously a freshly caught fish. He went on to explain that the river Tywi was a magnet for fishermen from all over the world. Famous names such as Pierce Brosnan have been seen in these parts, not to mention the former US President, Jimmy Carter, who is a frequent visitor, a fact confirmed by Huw who recalled being summoned to the Lampeter area to take his photograph with the world-famous fisherman, Moc Morgan.

As lunch progressed, the talk inevitably turned to rugby. Gareth and I compared the way our preparations were so different from the ways things operated in the 1970s. As is the norm when Alun Wyn Bevan is around, we were then asked to name our best Rugby World Cup XV made up of players who had competed in the final rounds of the competition since it was set up in 1987.

Gareth had no hesitation in naming the backs – he was in his element singing the praises of Blanco, Kirwan, Sella, Horan, Campese, Lomu, Lynagh, Larkham, Wilkinson, van der Westhuizen, Farr-Jones and Gregan. I chose John Eales and Martin Johnson as my second-row forwards; what a combination! There was some argument regarding the back row trio before we settled on Richard Hill, Buck Shelford and Michael Jones. Come to think of it, we never discussed the front row – there will have to be another lunch!

With the team sheet filled in it was time to head for the river. As we were about to leave the Polyn, we met up with Huw Tregelles Williams, renowned organist and former head of the BBC's music department in Wales, and Dr Terry James, a celebrated conductor and musical scholar (and, more interestingly for me, a great friend of the actor Richard Harris). Dr Terry was a charismatic character and we were left rolling about in laughter at the stories he had to tell. I would like to have stayed on to listen to some more but the river beckoned.

Gareth had by now changed into his fishing gear; the waistcoat to keep all his bits and pieces, the waders, the tweed cap and the most impressive fishing rod I have ever seen. I watched for about ten minutes as he skilfully tied the fly onto the hook. Then the line was cast again and again onto the fast flowing waters. As with any craft or sport, the best always make things look so easy, as I soon found out when it came to my turn. But by the end of the session, thanks to Gareth's tuition and patience, I felt that I had not made a complete idiot of myself and left determined to take up the pastime in the future. As we left I was encouraged by Gareth's parting words, 'Remember Alun – you're based in Hamilton for the World Cup. If you have a day off, Rotorua is just down the road and it's a great centre for fishing!' What a day it had been – fit for a King!

'You cast it, I'll catch it.'

'Welcome to the World Cup, mate.'
A traditional Maori greeting.

SEPTEMBER: Rugby World Cup I

A dip in the pool

Time to make bold predictions I think. Time to name the two teams from each World Cup pool who will progress to the quarter-finals!

Pool A:

Canada, France, Japan, New Zealand, Tonga.

Never underestimate the Canadians. Some of you might remember that they reached the quarter-final stage in 1991 before losing pluckily to the All Blacks at Lille by 29–13. Tonga will once again provide stiff opposition, Japan will most probably score some spectacular tries, but one has to say that New Zealand and France will comfortably reach the final stages. The All Blacks encounter against the *Tricolores* could prove interesting!

Pool B:

Argentina, England, Georgia, Romania, Scotland

Argentina were the surprise package of the 2007 competition, coming third behind eventual winners South Africa and England. Most critics would see them qualifying with England for the last eight, but don't write off Scotland. They are the only British and Irish team to have qualified for every quarter-final since the inaugural year and nearly made it to the final in 1991, eventually losing to England in the semi-final by the narrowest of margins. They'll have to compete without my Ospreys team-mate Nikki Walker, who was stretchered off against Italy at Murrayfield with medial ligament damage. Georgia will also be a force up-front having given the Irish the fright of their lives in a memorable match at Bordeaux in the 2007 competition. Ireland won 14–10 but my abiding memories of the encounter remain with the eastern Europeans camped on the Irish goal line in the dying minutes.

Pool C:

Australia, Ireland, Italy, Russia, United States

The group has a strong Welsh connection with Kingsley Jones, Darren Morris and Huw Wiltshire involved with the Russian squad, and Jarrad Griffiths from Pontardulais employed as an analyst with the USA Eagles. Australia and Ireland are everyone's favourites to proceed but the Italians, having defeated France in this year's Six Nations and coming mightily close to defeating Ireland, must be respected.

Pool D:

Fiji, Namibia, Samoa, South Africa, Wales

This is certainly the toughest group in the competition with Fiji, Samoa and South Africa confident of success. Our game against Samoa will be a key fixture. Our preparations will be meticulous and I can state unequivocally that the team will focus on all aspects of play with the sole intention of winning. South Africa and Wales to qualify from this pool!

Sunday, September 11th, 2011 sees the start of the Rugby World Cup for Wales and I, like every other Welshman in the team, will be concentrating my efforts entirely on trying to defeat South Africa at Wellington. However, in the hours leading up to kick-off, I will also be thinking of the victims and families of the 9/11 massacre. It's the tenth anniversary of the attack on the World Trade Centre towers on the bank of the East River in New York City. At the time I was a 15-year-old schoolboy at Bishop Gore Comprehensive and was informed of the catastrophe at school. I eventually returned home to watch the horrifying images on television.

September 11

South Africa v Wales (Wellington Regional Stadium)

Disappointed – obviously; proud – most certainly. This was a magnificent performance by Wales; we as players knew it, the opposition knew it and every knowledgeable rugby supporter knew it. Even our sternest critics had to acknowledge that the team who lost deserved to win. We were totally devastated at the final whistle because we knew that the game was there for the taking. Every player deserves to be praised. There have been some pretty impressive performances by Wales during the game's history and this was up there with the best of them. The forward effort in all aspects of play was exemplary whilst the backs played their part in causing constant problems for the Springboks defence.

As a playing member it's not my intention to criticise referees for crucial decisions. We'll certainly make our personal feelings known within four walls but I have to admit that I was amazed that Wayne Barnes (who is one of my favourite officials) didn't seek advice from the television match official during that infamous James Hook penalty goal. I noticed that he waited patiently for confirmation prior to François Steyn and Toby Faletau's tries when both efforts seemed clear cut scores.

More spring than the Springbok. Taking Huw Bennett's pinpoint throw, with a lot of help from Luke Charteris (wearing scrum cap) and Toby Faletau.

Another three points for James Hook.
Not according to referee Wayne Barnes.

'This is how you do it, Shane.' About to dance my way past South Africa's Schalk Burger (7), watched by a seated Fourie Du Preez (9), a reclining Shane Williams, and an upright Paul James and John Smit.

Toby Faletau scores Wales's first try of Rugby World Cup 2011

I remember reading that Carwyn James, the coach of the successful '71 Lions had remarked after a Lions defeat in the second test match in New Zealand, 'I now know we can win the series!' And after our narrow defeat to South Africa, we the players can also say, 'We can win it!' The feeling in the camp prior, during and after the match was one of complete unity. It's not usual to see bench players being vociferous. They're usually quietly waiting for their opportunity to take someone's place but apparently Andy Powell was on his feet shouting words of encouragement. That's the spirit which wins competitions.

In the post-match discussions I took umbrage with François Pienaar and Justin Marshall's statements claiming Wales lacked courage to win big matches. The only reason they are questioning our belief is due to their own insecurities. They seem determined to make outlandish comments so as to justify their very presence as critics. There was no missing ingredient – all the stats proved we played exceptionally well. I can assure you that we'll learn from that defeat. We have the momentum to go into the next game with confidence knowing we have the potential to be giant killers.

South Africa: F Steyn, Pietersen, Fourie, de Villiers (James 24'), Habana (Hougaard 61'), M Steyn, du Preez, Mtawarira (Steenkamp 55'), Smit (c) (B du Plessis 57'), J du Plessis, Rossouw, Matfield (Muller 45'), Brussow, Spiers (Alberts 57'), Burger Not used: van der Linde.	**Wales:** Hook, North, J Davies, Roberts, Shane Williams, Priestland, Phillips, James, Bennett, Adam Jones, Charteris, AW Jones (Bradley Davies 67'), Lydiate, Faletau, Warburton (c) Not used: Burns, Bevington, Powell, Knoyle, Scott Williams, Halfpenny.

South Africa 17 F Steyn (t), Hougaard (t), M Steyn (2c, 1pg)

Wales **16** Faletau (t), Hook (c, 3pg)

Referee: Wayne Barnes (RFU)	**Attendance:** 34,500

Huge Bennett! My Ospreys team-mate Huw Bennett proved heroic at the World Cup. Here he secures possession under the nose of South Africa's John Smit.

On the morning of the match, my agent phoned me, desperately seeking a ticket for the actor James Nesbitt, who was in New Zealand filming *The Hobbit*. He's a huge rugby fan so I was glad to be of assistance. What's more, he actually ended up watching the game with the WAGs and families of the Welsh players!

September 16

There have been some horrendous catastrophies worldwide during the year, and it was with great sadness that we as a squad learnt of the loss of lives at the Gleision Colliery at Cilybebyll near Pontardawe.

Although we're based on the other side of the world, news filters through quickly as a result of modern technology. As Welshmen, we've been brought up on tales of mining tragedies. We all thought that those days were long gone but sadly that is no longer the case. As a squad, we were all devastated by the news and couldn't stop thinking of the consequences for the families involved and the community in the Swansea valley.

It was a tragic end to a dramatic search for the trapped miners. Rescuers, who must be congratulated for their heroic efforts, discovered the last of the miners after two days of searching the colliery's labyrinth of tunnels. We can't even imagine what David Powell, Phillip Hill, Charles Breslin and Garry Jenkins had been through. As Peter Hain, the local Member of Parliament for the area said, 'It was a stab through the heart of the local community. We have seen extraordinary courage by the families in tortuous hours of waiting.'

'A little bit higher, Luke.' Mike Phillips (right) smiles and Luke Charteris lifts, as I stretch every sinew to win line-out ball against Samoa.

September 18

Samoa v Wales (Waikato Stadium, Hamilton)

It was a win or bust scenario. Lose, and we were well aware that we would be out of the competition. During the last 130 years Wales has managed to play an attractive, often thrilling brand of rugby which has pleased and impressed rugby purists from all over the globe. The win against Samoa wasn't pretty but mightily effective and might well result in a potential quarter-final clash with Ireland at Wellington on October 8. At last the Samoan Rugby World Cup ghosts had been well and truly banished!

Samoa are a very good side. Underestimate them at your peril. Their recent victory against Australia caused the rugby world at large to stand up and take note. They have impressed many in previous World Cups but it's true to say that the current squad is by far the best and most experienced to have represented the Pacific Island team. Most of the team play in highly competitive leagues in England and France, whilst scrum-half Kahn Fotuali'i and back row forward George Stowers will be joining the Ospreys for this forthcoming campaign.

We were extremely disappointed to have conceded a try at the end of a physical and confrontational first half, but you could say that they deserved their interval lead. We had one or two chances but failed to take advantage whilst Samoa controlled the territory and waited patiently for opportunities. The second half saw a far more composed Welsh team who imposed pressure, thanks to some pretty astute game management strategies. We stretched the opposition and managed to keep ball in hand which is so important in the modern game. We certainly had the upper hand, with the side's character and belief coming to the fore. I was delighted to have received the Man of the Match accolade in such a vital contest.

A worrying sight. Dan Lydiate leaves the field with physio Mark Davies (left) and team doctor Professor John Williams.

Sam Warburton (left) watches Shane Williams
and Samoa's Anitelea Tuilagi in full flight!

Jonathan Davies hurdling his way over the Samoan tacklers, with George North right behind him.

However the try was an example of the magic which has been such an important part of our heritage – Leigh Halfpenny somehow got back on to his feet in a desperate situation near his own 22, evaded the clutches of two or three would be attackers and sprinted for the opposition try line all of 70 metres away. He was aided by the enthusiastic Jonathan Davies and when the final pass went astray it was Shane Williams who scooped up the bouncing ball and nonchalantly crossed the line. Game, set and match!

It was a weekend, however, where events back home weren't too far from our minds. I was pleased that Warren Gatland had pledged support on our behalf to the families of the Gleision Colliery disaster, and that our captain Sam Warburton dedicated our victory to the memory of the four miners. However, as a squad, we were disappointed that the authorities refused our request for a minute's silence prior to kick-off.

Wales: Hook (Halfpenny 40'), North, Jonathan Davies, Roberts, Shane Williams, Priestland, Phillips, P James (Jenkins 61'), Bennett (Burns 61'), Adam Jones, Charteris, AW Jones (B Davies 68'), Lydiate (Powell 9'), Faletau, Warburton (c)	**Samoa:** P Williams, Tagicakibau (So'oialo 55'), Pisi, Mapusua (Sapolu-Fuimaono 69'), Alesana Tuilagi, Lavea (Su'a 68'), Fotuali'i, Taulafo, Schwalger (c) (Paulo 72'), Perenise (Johnston 69'), Leo (Tekori 68'), Thompson, Treviranus (Salavea 76'), Stowers, Faasavalu
Samoa 10 Perenise (t), Williams (pg, c)	
Wales 17 Shane Williams (t), Hook (2pg), Priestland (2pg)	
Referee: Alain Rolland (IRFU)	**Attendance:** 25,800

September 26

Namibia v Wales (Stadium Taranaki, New Plymouth)

Job done! A bonus point, twelve tries and 81 points to boost our points aggregate. However, our coaches weren't exactly happy individuals at half time – Warren was livid and Robert Howley was furious! We started superbly, scoring three tries in the opening quarter, but then for some reason took our foot off the pedal and allowed Namibia back into the match. It was totally unacceptable and out of character and we, as players, accepted the harsh words spoken in the dressing room at half-time and went out to redeem the situation.

The second half saw a revitalised Welsh team who totally outplayed Namibia in all aspects of the game. Some critics felt that Wales should have fielded their strongest side for the fixture in order to allow players to become accustomed to each other. It's the philosophy of 'The more you play together, the better you get.' But injuries and decisions to experiment with various line-ups don't always allow coaches to be conservative. The pleasing aspect of the Namibian match was the determination and quality exemplified by the players who were making their first appearance in the competition. In the past, it's been said that Wales has a first-class first team but very little strength to fall back on. That is certainly not the case anymore.

It was a commanding performance to celebrate Stephen Jones's 101st cap but there were other interesting facts to please the anoraks amongst you. George North (and what a handful he is) became the youngest try scorer (19 years and 166 days) in the history of Rugby World Cup, breaking the record set by Joe Roff of Australia in 1999. Ken Owens became the first player since Jason Jones-Hughes in 1999 to make his international debut in a Rugby World Cup match. And the final try, scored by yours truly, was Wales's hundredth try in the competition.

Namibia: Botha, Van Wyk, Van Zyl, De La Harpe (Philander), Dames (TC Losper), Kotze, Jantjies, Redelinghuys (Larson), Hugo Horn, Jané Du Toit, Heinz Koll, Nico Esterhuyse, Tinus Du Plessis, Nieuwenhuis, Burger (c)	**Wales:** Byrne, Halfpenny, J Davies, Scott Williams, Brew (North 56'), S Jones (Priestland 64'), Knoyle (Ll Williams 59'), Jenkins (Bevington 62'), Burns (Owens) 62', Mitchell, B Davies, AW Jones, R Jones, Faletau (Charteris 56'), Warburton (c) (Powell 48')
Namibia 7 Koll (t), Kotze (c)	
Wales 81 Scott Williams (3t), Brew (t), Falatau (t), Jenkins (t), North (2t), J Davies (t), Ll Williams (t), Byrne (t), AW Jones (t), S Jones (1pg, 6c), Priestland (3c)	
Referee: Steve Walsh (ARFU)	**Attendance:** 14,710

Jet prop-elled! Gethin Jenkins sprints away for his try against Namibia, urged on by (from the left) Ryan Jones, Andy Powell, AWJ and Bradley Davies.

Great, Scott! Look who's in (distant) support again as hat-trick hero Scott Williams splits the Namibian defence.

Replacement scrum-half Lloyd Williams
joins in the try spree against Namibia.

October 2

Fiji v Wales (Waikato Stadium, Hamilton)

Let's not get excited. Let's not get ahead of ourselves. A month ago most critics were unsure whether we'd get past South Africa and Samoa in the group stage but now those same people are tipping us to get to the final. It's a mad, mad world! However, we might have cruised into the last eight of the Rugby World Cup but as yet we haven't achieved anything. Other Welsh teams, in 1999 and 2003, reached the quarter-final stages and eventually lost out to Australia and England respectively. I know it's a cliché but from now on, it really is 'one game at a time'.

We certainly managed to lay the ghost of 2007 with a comprehensive victory over the Fijians, scoring nine tries in the process in front of a 28,800 crowd at Hamilton. The islanders had their supporters but so did we thanks to a partisan and vociferous Welsh contingent, along with thousands of locals who were present to support Warren, whose family home is just down the road from the stadium. Yes, we were pretty impressive and clinical in most aspects of the game. Whilst the majority of fans complimented us on the 66 points scored, our defence coach Shaun Edwards was more than pleased with the zero on the scoreboard next to the word FIJI! They had their hour of glory in Nantes in 2007; it was now our turn to celebrate. The 7UP and Pepsis flowed in Hamilton on Sunday evening – that's how motivated and disciplined we've become!

Wales's armchair critics, and they're in their thousands, have constantly uttered the phrase, 'We have no strength in depth.' I think that's been put to bed with our performances during the past month in New Zealand. One player gets injured and another comes along to provide Warren and his coaching team with major selection headaches prior to the next match. One player who'll certainly be playing against our Celtic cousins is George North, who has become a rugby sensation here in New Zealand as a result of his defence-splitting runs. He's being compared to Jonah Lomu by New Zealanders! However, whilst O'Driscoll and company try to work out methods of dealing with young George, there'll be fourteen others equally determined and focused to cross the Irish try line. We created one opportunity during our Grand Slam victory at Croke Park in 2008 and came away with a deserved victory. We intend to repeat that success on Saturday, October 8 at Wellington.

Fiji: Keresoni, Vulivuli (Goneva 68'), Fatiaki, Lovobalavu (Bai 55'), Tagicakibau, Little, Buatava (Kenatale 76'), Talei (c), Matadigo, Nasiga (Ravulo 61'), Lewaravu, Nakarawa, Somoca (Ma'afu 51'), Nailago (Qera 65'), Koto Vuli (Veikoso 40')

Wales: Byrne, North, Scott Williams, Roberts (J Davies 65'), Halfpenny, Priestland (S Jones 58'), Phillips (Ll Williams 54'), Jenkins, Bennett (Burns 35'), A Jones (James 58'), B Davies (AW Jones 40'), Charteris, R Jones, Faletau (Powell 53'), Warburton (c)

Fiji   0

Wales 66 Scott Williams (t), Roberts (2t), North (t), Warburton (t), Burns (t), Halfpenny (t), Ll Williams (t), J Davies (t), Priestland (1pg, 5c), S Jones (4c)

Referee: Wayne Barnes (RFU)   **Attendance:** 28,800

'Go north, young man!' Fiji tacklers are left sprawling in the wake of tournament sensation George North.

'I'm right behind you, skip.' Sam Warburton about to show Fiji (and me) a clean pair of heels.

'Engage. Pause. Touch.' Wales's second-string front row get it wrong in the rain!

'Touch. Pause. Engage.'
Wales's front row (from left) Adam Jones, Huw Bennett and Gethin Jenkins about to meet their Fijian counterparts, with Mike Phillips above them, Toby Faletau behind them and Ryan Jones at their side.

One Welshman, three Irishmen. The odds are stacked in Jamie Roberts's favour, as Brian O'Driscoll, Stephen Ferris (with scrum cap) and a prone Donncha O'Callaghan find out to their cost. Mike Phillips looks on approvingly.

OCTOBER:
Rugby World Cup II

The knock-out blow

October 8

Rugby World Cup Quarter-final Ireland v Wales (Wellington Regional Stadium)

It was a stunning victory. The critics were full of praise and rightly so because on the day we proved superior to a very good Irish side in all aspects of the game. I know I'm only 26 years of age but of the games I've played it was the one match which gave me the most satisfaction because it constituted a near perfect performance.

I'm not one to spend hours poring over the sports pages on a Sunday morning and I detest the column inches devoted by some journalists to providing marks out of ten for individual performances. However, on this occasion, such a statistical record could have been completed in seconds – ten out of ten for all my fellow players in red jerseys. I'd also like to give the same mark to the other bench players and trusted team-mates sitting in the stand whose enthusiastic support and camaraderie was equally appreciated.

I suppose that Ireland came into the match feeling that they had a slight psychological advantage. After all they were accomplished performers who knew how to clinch victories in trying circumstances. The Leinster and Munster contingent had, at regular intervals, won Heineken Cup Finals when the chips were down and the men in green had also won the Grand Slam in 2009.

However, we as an unit (and I include our superb coaching team) were quietly confident of success. Our preparations had been meticulous and our game plan logged in our memory banks. Even when Ireland retaliated with Keith Earls' try we weren't in the least bit fazed. Mike Phillips's try was so typical of the man – Gareth Edwards, Terry Holmes and Robert Howley would have been in their seventh heavens! And from then on in it was all Wales. And there was no happier man in Wellington than the iconic All Black second-row forward, Colin Meads, who had not only predicted

No half measures from Leigh Halfpenny as he kicks this penalty goal against Ireland from the halfway line.

a Welsh victory but had also been so complimentary of our style of play. The Irish lads were full of praise in defeat with Rory Best predicting further Welsh success in the semi-final against France. It was a day to remember.

Ireland: Kearney, Bowe, O'Driscoll (c), D'Arcy, Earls (Trimble 70'), O'Gara (Sexton 55'), Murray (Reddan 55'), Healy, Best, Ross, O'Callaghan, O'Connell, Ferris (Leamy 74'), Heaslip (Ryan 74'), O'Brien	**Wales:** Halfpenny, North, J Davies, Roberts, Shane Williams, Priestland (Hook 77'), Phillips, Jenkins, Bennett, A Jones, Charteris (B Davies 40'), AW Jones, Lydiate, Faletau, Warburton (c)
Ireland 10 Earls (t), O'Gara (1pg, 1c)	
Wales 25 Shane Williams (t), Phillips (t), Jonathan Davies (t), Priestland (1pg, 2c), Halfpenny (1pg)	
Referee: Craig Joubert (South Africa)	**Attendance:** 35,787

October 9

We haven't won anything yet and we have to be wary of what we want to do. We have got to look at it as though there are still three or four games left to go, rather than just two . . . The problem is that we tend to get ahead of ourselves as Welsh people and as a Welsh nation. We have got to look at it as one game at a time – if we don't we will slip up.

We will front up tomorrow, make sure everyone is fit, do our recovery and then get into the working week. Then we will address who we have to play. We need to keep the work rate and the accuracy in our game and we will see what happens. We had the utmost respect for Ireland after the performances they had put in during the pool stages. The young players coming in are a credit to themselves and the squad.

The ball is there to be used and we didn't want to shy away from playing a bit of rugby as we had done in the pool stages.

Brother in arms on his knees.
My second-row partner Luke Charteris receiving treatment from physio Prav Mathema.

Jonathan Davies on his way to the try line.

Deja vu!
Mike Phillips dives over in the left-hand corner against Ireland once again.

Wales's heroic captain Sam Warburton,
leaves the field against France,
desolate but dignified.

October 15

Rugby World Cup Semi-final France v Wales (Eden Park, Auckland)

We started as favourites and felt confident in our ability to control the match and progress to the final of Rugby World Cup 2011. It was not to be. Our tight-head prop, Adam Jones, left the field after nine minutes play with a calf injury, and our captain Sam Warburton was controversially shown a red card by referee Alain Rolland following a spear tackle on Vincent Clerc. The International Rugby Board's directive on spear tackles is worth quoting. If the tackle is up in the air above the horizontal then it is encumbent on the tackler to ensure that the tackled player lands safely. Now whilst I agree that Sam Warburton's initial contact was 'above the horizontal' he then made every effort to release his grip and ensure that the Toulouse wing three-quarter came to ground unimpeded.

Having seen the incident on numerous occasions, I am totally convinced that Sam's initial thrust was not malicious but could be construed as dangerous. It constituted a spear tackle, but his determination to withdraw from the situation and allow Clerc to land safely did in my opinion not merit the red card. Some would say that Alain Rolland's decision ruined a potentially great contest but that's not the point. A misdemeanour should be punished with the same consistency whether it's a 3rd XV fixture at Mumbles or a World Cup Final. It seems unjust that Tongan wing Sukanaivalu Hufanga was yellow carded by Steve Walsh for upending Vincent Clerc during his team's 19–14 pool win against France, whilst Sam got a red from Rolland for the same offence. I fervently believe that the sending off was unfortunate and I wish that the referee had spoken to his assistants and asked the vital question, 'Did the tackler withdraw prior to the recipient landing on the ground?' I wonder whether the referee made an objective assessment of the overall circumstances of the tackle?

Most rugby followers must have thought that it was all over. To have to play for three quarters of the game with fourteen players is a tall order, but as players we decided to get on with it and give our all. In trying circumstances we battled resolutely and even managed to secure our own ball in scrummages when the chips were really down. Unfortunately two kickable penalties were missed early on but our efforts in the last twenty minutes of the first half gave us enough confidence to persevere and fight to the bitter end.

A magician among giants. Lionel Nallet (5) watches Shane Williams cast another spell, as Luke Charteris looks down from on high, and Huw Bennett (2) holds up his hands.

Welsh determination is etched on Jamie Roberts's face, as he tries to get past Imanol Harinordoquy. George North looks ahead, confident that Jamie will succeed.

A giant leap for Welsh rugby.
Though I jump higher, my
opposite number Lionel
Nallet gets there before me.
It was a disappointing night
for the Welsh line-out.

Bye, bye, Pape.
Mike Phillips brushes off Pascal Pape before going on to score the game's only try, watched by Huw Bennett.

Faletau at full tilt!
Number eight Toby Faletau makes another incisive run, with Gethin Jenkins in support,
and France's Dimitri Szarzewski (in white boots) and Thierry Dusautoir (far right) in pursuit.

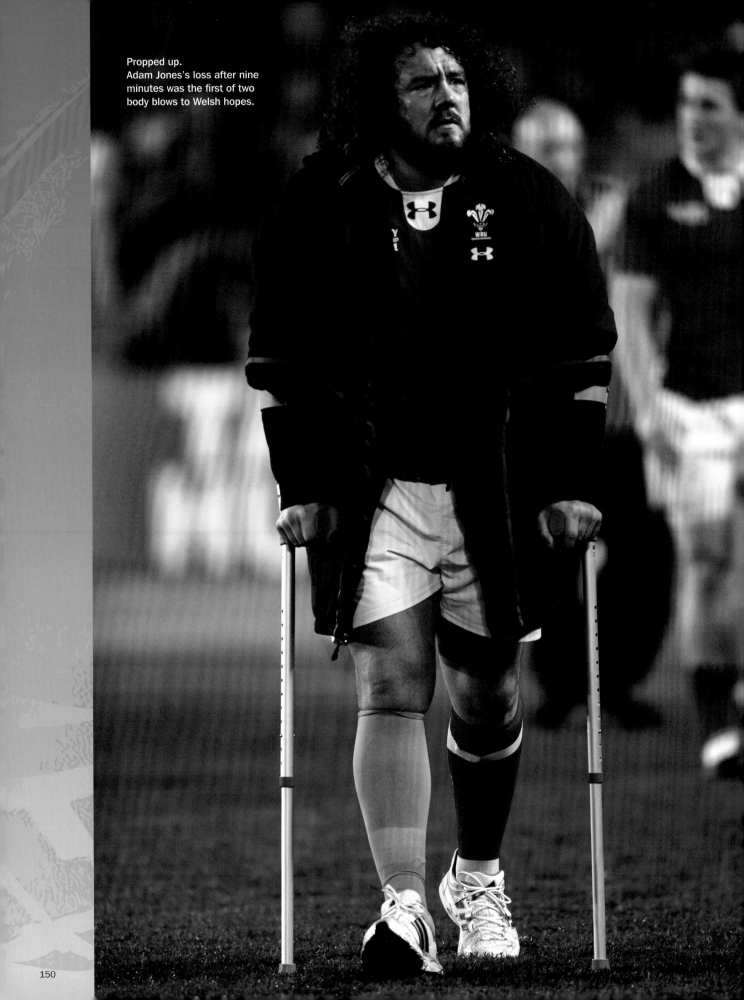

Propped up.
Adam Jones's loss after nine minutes was the first of two body blows to Welsh hopes.

I must say that the second half performance was truly outstanding against one of the finest forward combinations in the competition. Mike's try was just the tonic we required and if Stephen's conversion had been a few inches to the right it could have put us into the lead. Our heads never dropped – Leigh's monster effort against the wind from halfway dropped inches under the bar and then Stephen wasn't given the time and space to drop back into the pocket for that all-important drop goal. The final whistle led to anguish and tears; we were crestfallen in defeat having given so much to the game and the competition. It was heartbreaking.

France: Médard, Clerc, Rougerie, Mermoz, Palisson, Parra, Yachvili, Poux (Barcella 45'), Servat (Szarzewski 45'), Mas, Pape (Pierre 61'), Nallet, Dusautoir (c), Harinordoquy, Bonnaire (Quedraogo 72')

Wales: Halfpenny, North, J Davies, Roberts, Shane Williams, Hook (S Jones 46'), Phillips, Jenkins, Bennett, Adam Jones (P James 9'), Charteris, AW Jones (B Davies 61'), Lydiate (R Jones 55'), Faletau, Warburton (c)

France 9 Parra (3pg)

Wales 8 Hook (1pg) Phillips (t)

Referee: Alain Rolland (Ireland)   **Attendance:** 58,629

A study in disappointment.
To my left are a disconsolate Stephen Jones,
Bradley Davies and Dan Lydiate.

The 2011 World Cup also proved a coaching triumph for Warren Gatland and Shaun Edwards (left), not to mention the likes of Robert Howley and Robin McBryde.

October 21

Rugby World Cup Third Place Play-off Australia v Wales (Eden Park, Auckland)

It's early morning following our third place play-off defeat and I find it difficult putting pen to paper. Whilst waiting for our return flight to London Heathrow via Dubai, I caught a glimpse of websites which told me what the leading journalists had written. Paul Rees in *The Guardian* was spot on when he said that 'the play-off is a scrap for a prize no one wants'. He goes on to say that 'there is an element of cruelty to it, forcing players whose minds had drifted elsewhere to rouse themselves for a battle they do not have the heart for'.

I have no hesitation in stating that, on the day, the better side won. However, our final try was truly outstanding and a timely reminder of the rugby we'd played in the tournament. Australia controlled play throughout and deservedly collected their bronze medals at the final whistle. Some would say that we were psychologically and emotionally scarred as a result of our semi-final experience because our sole aim was to get to the final of Rugby World Cup 2011. Fourth place was not what he had in mind. James Lawton's piece in *The Independent* encapsulated our efforts – 'Welsh burnt out by brilliant efforts but the future is bright.' You bet it's bright!

Lawton was obviously won over by our style of play during the tournament. 'Even in the seconds before the final whistle they had reminded themselves of why in these last few weeks they have attracted so much praise, so much affection, and why Warren Gatland was later able to claim before them stretched not the pain of final defeat but the possibility of "huge development".'

Aussie winger James O'Connor kicks for goal, as Huw Bennett and Bradley Davies hope against hope.

It was a great day for Nathan Sharpe who became the third second-row forward in world rugby to reach a hundred caps following in the footsteps of Victor Matfield and Fabien Pelous. Surprisingly it was Australia's first victory at Eden Park since 1986. The final words to two Welsh journalists. Carolyn Hitt in the *Western Mail*, 'They may not be coming home with a trophy or medals but in the greater scheme of things they've won something just as precious – respect.' Thanks Carolyn, but in 2015 it's going to be respect and the Webb Ellis trophy! It proved to be an unbelievable adventure for us all, especially because of the incredible support from the people in New Zealand, as well as the Welsh public back home.

Australia: Beale (Horne 12'), O'Connor, Ashley-Cooper, Barnes, Ioane, Cooper (Anthony Fainga'a 21'), Genia (Burgess 67'), Slipper, Polota Nau (Saia Fainga'a 52'), Ma'afu (Alexander 60'), Horwill (c) (Samo 71'), Sharpe (Simmons 45'), Higginbotham (Samo temp 30-33'), McCalman, Pocock

Wales: Halfpenny, North (S Jones temp 33-37), Jonathan Davies (Scott Williams 70'), Roberts, Shane Williams, Hook (S Jones 50'), Phillips (Ll Williams 63'), Jenkins (c), Bennett (Burns 70'), James (Bevington 63'), B Davies, Charteris (AW Jones 53'), Lydiate (Powell 63'), R Jones, Faletau

Australia 21 Barnes (t, 1dg), McCalman (t), O'Connor (2pg, 1c)

Wales   18 Shane Williams (t), Halfpenny (t), Hook (1pg), S Jones (1pg, 1c)

Referee: Wayne Barnes (RFU)   **Attendance:** 53,243

Shane's last international try away from home.

What next? Shane Williams contemplates the immediate future, as the Welsh squad, including Gethin Jenkins and Lloyd Burns, show appreciation of the incredible support we received in New Zealand.

'Mark!' One of the stars of Rugby World Cup 2011, New Zealand full-back Israel Dagg, comes on in leaps and bounds.

POSTSCRIPT

October 23

New Zealand 8 France 7. I heard the result of the World Cup Final whilst travelling from Dubai to Heathrow. Not surprised that France took up the challenge and came close to defeating the All Blacks – you just never know with the *Tricolores*!

Anyway, October or not, that's my World Cup year at an end. A year of ups and downs, but one that may well be seen in the future as the year which launched another golden age for Welsh rugby. Whether this is the case will depend on how all players and rugby folk in Wales respond to the challenge thrown down by the 2011 Rugby World Cup.

So, for me, it's back to the Ospreys, and back to the training paddock. But I genuinely believe that rugby in Wales is in better hands and in a better place than we thought possible at one time

Kicker of the World-Cup-winning penalty goal, Stephen Donald, fourth-choice fly half turned national hero.

Woodcock-a-hoop! A nation celebrates as Tony Woodcock dives over for New Zealand's only try in the 2011 Rugby World Cup final, ushered over by his fellow forwards.

ACKNOWLEDGEMENTS

With thanks to everyone who generously gave of their time for such a worthy cause, all refusing to accept payment for their services. These included Ben Evans, James Pinniger and Colorsport, Gareth Everett, Gareth Edwards, Iolo Williams, Helen Randle Photography, Gareth Criddle and the management at Stratstone in Cardiff, Andy Rouse Wildlife Photographer, Phill Davies Photography in Aberaeron, Emyr Evans and the Dyfi Osprey project team.

We would also like to thank Gomer Press in Llandysul and in particular Ceri Wyn Jones for his guidance, patience and enthusiasm in formulating the publication. The cause is a deserving one. Most of us at some time have witnessed friends and family suffering from, and sometimes succumbing to, this killer disease. Most importantly let's also remind ourselves that thousands upon thousands are also recovering from cancer as a result of medical expertise and research programmes funded the world over.

Alun Wyn Jones, Huw Evans and Alun Wyn Bevan